Family Walks and Hikes
of Vancouver Island

Volume 1

Family Walks and Hikes of Vancouver Island

Volume 1
Victoria to Nanaimo

REVISED EDITION

THEO DOMBROWSKI

RMB

For information on purchasing bulk quantities of this book, or to obtain media excerpts or invite the author to speak at an event, please visit rmbooks.com and select the "Contact" tab.

RMB | Rocky Mountain Books Ltd.
rmbooks.com
@rmbooks
facebook.com/rmbooks

Cataloguing data available from Library and Archives Canada
ISBN 9781771604031 (softcover)
ISBN 9781771604048 (electronic)

All photographs are by Theo Dombrowski unless otherwise noted.

Cover photos: Mossy Branches in West Coast Rainforest © iStock.com/GlowingEarth, Backpackers Examine an Edible Orange Mushroom while Hiking Through Forest © iStock.com/PamelaJoeMcFarlane

Printed and bound in China

We would like to also take this opportunity to acknowledge the traditional territories upon which we live and work. In Calgary, Alberta, we acknowledge the Niitsitapi (Blackfoot) and the people of the Treaty 7 region in Southern Alberta, which includes the Siksika, the Piikuni, the Kainai, the Tsuut'ina and the Stoney Nakoda First Nations, including Chiniki, Bearpaw, and Wesley First Nations. The City of Calgary is also home to Métis Nation of Alberta, Region III. In Victoria, British Columbia, we acknowledge the traditional territories of the Lkwungen (Esquimalt, and Songhees), Malahat, Pacheedaht, Scia'new, T'Sou-ke and W̱SÁNEĆ(Pauquachin, Tsartlip, Tsawout, Tseycum) peoples.

We acknowledge the financial support of the Government of Canada through the Canada Book Fund and the Canada Council for the Arts, and of the province of British Columbia through the British Columbia Arts Council and the Book Publishing Tax Credit.

Disclaimer

The actions described in this book may be considered inherently dangerous activities. Individuals undertake these activities at their own risk. The information put forth in this guide has been collected from a variety of sources and is not guaranteed to be completely accurate or reliable. Many conditions and some information may change owing to weather and numerous other factors beyond the control of the authors and publishers. Individuals or groups must determine the risks, use their own judgment, and take full responsibility for their actions. Do not depend on any information found in this book for your own personal safety. Your safety depends on your own good judgment based on your skills, education and experience.

It is up to the users of this guidebook to acquire the necessary skills for safe experiences and to exercise caution in potentially hazardous areas. The author and publisher of this guide accept no responsibility for your actions or the results that occur from another's actions, choices or judgments. If you have any doubt as to your safety or your ability to attempt anything described in this guidebook, do not attempt it.

CONTENTS

AREA MAP

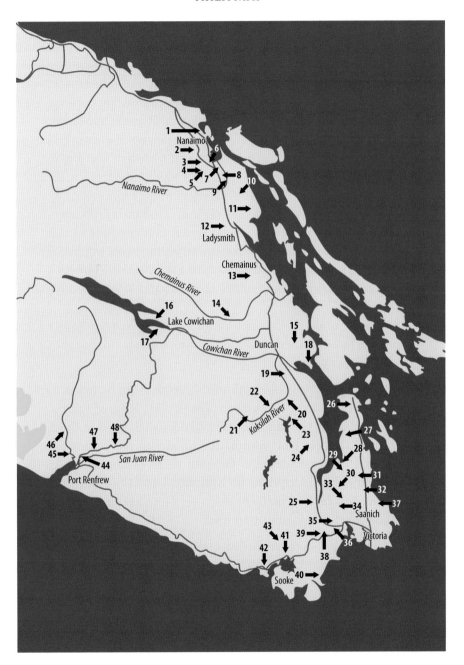

Nanaimo
1
2
3
4
5 6 7 8 10
9
Nanaimo River
11
12 Ladysmith
Chemainus
13
Chemainus River
16 14
Lake Cowichan
17
Cowichan River Duncan
15
18
19
22
21 Koksilah River 20
23
24
26
27
28
29
30 31
33 32
25 34 37
35 Saanich
43 41 39
42 38 36 Victoria
40
Sooke
47 48
46
45 44
San Juan River
Port Renfrew

INTRODUCTION

Family Hikes

What makes a perfectly normal hike a "family hike"? There is, of course, no simple answer. We all have a pretty good idea of what doesn't belong in a book of family walks and hikes on Vancouver Island. A stroll through the beds of spring flowers in Beacon Hill Park is not what most families are looking for when wanting to take their brood for a dollop of nature walking. And they would blanch at the suggestion of assembling climbing ropes and heaving themselves *en famille* up the cliffs of 2200-m Mt. Elkhorn. No doubt, there are toddlers who would find the Beacon Hill Park option overwhelming and some strapping teens would call Mt. Elkhorn a jolly romp. Between these extremes, however, there is a rough middle ground that includes a considerable range of possibilities.

Unsurprisingly, the family outings in this book are as hugely varied as families themselves. Still, they correspond, roughly, to the following four principles:

1. Nothing in this book duplicates walks that can be found in *Seashore Walks of Vancouver* or *Popular Day Hikes of Vancouver Island*, by the same author and publisher. Both of those books have lots of information on walks and hikes that would be great for some families: these can be culled by reading the descriptions for difficulty, length and elevation gain. In addition, many of the trails described in this book you won't find in any other book.

2. All the trails here have a "natural" setting. Many fine walks in other books wind through city streets, along harbour fronts and so on. The trails in this book stick more or less to the woods. Admittedly, a few are surprisingly close to city streets: Millstone Creek Park in Nanaimo, for example, is surrounded by streets. It, however, and a few others

perilously close to city streets, are sufficiently large and full of ungroomed forest to create that sense of *Ahh* that comes with release from concrete and cars and the *Ooh* that comes with encountering huge old trees and gurgling streams.

3. Every trip in this book includes something special for children. Adults can be perfectly pleased walking sedately along a path that does nothing more than wind amongst second-growth forest. Children often have a hard time feeling such pleasure. They want an element of fun, surprise, thrill or the extraordinary. And who can blame them? Thus, each of the entries in this book comes accompanied by notes on what children might find interesting. The key word, of course, is "might." Nothing is less guaranteed in this world than a child's interest.

Still, many children perk up when water hoves into view, especially if there is a chance – with or without parental approval – of interacting with the water. And the good news? A high proportion of the trails in this book link to streams, rivers or lakes. Of course, amongst watery delights, the mighty waterfall probably is the most fascinating. Not surprisingly, then, many of the trails in this book lead to waterfalls, some famous, some so obscure as to be known only by locals, but all of them impressive.

A word of warning: Many waterfalls can be viewed securely only from the top of a ravine. A good deal of parental judgment and care will necessarily go into assessing how much latitude to give the eager-beaver child who wants to go just…that…little…bit…farther.

On the other hand, most children are notoriously immune to the charm of The Pretty View. More good news: nearly all the trails in this book that lead up hills don't just provide a pretty view but also have something else – that airy king-of-the-castle excitement that comes from cliffy heights or (safe) rocky bluffs for clambering, or, of course, the perfect picnic spot.

Likewise, it's hard to pin down what will spark each individual child's interest in the natural world. What about huge, swarming ant hills, woodpecker trees, beaver lodges, spawning salmon, nesting herons or vulture-updraft cliffs? You will find such features in the trail descriptions. The wily parent will use this information to whip up a little anticipation. The same wily parent can create eagerness about features that make viewing wildlife interesting – raised viewing platforms, suspended walkways, colourful interpretative signs.

No matter how fascinating nature walks are for some children, however, some simply don't like walking. Why walk, they wonder, when they can scoot about on two wheels? For such children (and, possibly, their parents), included in this book is information on which trails are suitable both for two feet and for bicycles (with, in most cases, sturdy tires).

Above all, and, indeed, in addition to all is that all-time highlight of any family expedition into the woods: the picnic! Although sandwiches and cookies can be devoured anywhere, knowing in advance about specific spots, and even picnic tables, can make planning a family outing huge fun.

4. No suitable parks have been omitted, but many of the trails are not in parks. It might seem unnecessary to direct parents to public parks that are, after all, public. This is especially the case with such high-profile parks as Mt. Douglas or Little Qualicum Falls. The fact is, however, knowing in advance exactly the best places to begin a walk, what facilities to expect, and, even more important, the trails within a park that are often overlooked that can transform a ho-hum walk into a memorable family outing.

    If the park you select is provincial, be a little more guarded than if it is national, regional district or municipal. While regional and municipal parks have increasingly shown impressive flurries of energy – new parks, new trails and new facilities popping up everywhere – sadly, the same is not true of provincial parks. Some are well-served, of course, particularly if there is a popular cash-generating campsite associated with them. Many, however, are strikingly undeveloped or neglected. Broken boardwalks, faded signs, collapsed and eroded trails suggest that the provincial government has had different spending priorities.

Many of the best nature walks and hikes are mostly known only to locals. Look at the entries, for example, for Chemainus Lake, Koksilah Trails and Yellow Point Bog Ecological Reserve – and you may realize that at least some of these have largely escaped your attention and your planning for a family outing.

Parks contain only a fraction of the trails on Vancouver Island. Outside of them, Vancouver Island is aswarm with trails – more trails than could fit into any book. Horse riders, walkers and mountain bikers have converted old deer trails, abandoned logging roads and just plain old wilderness into an astounding network of winding ways. Only a tiny selection of these trails is included in this book. These are the ones that, rather than just satisfy the interests of local users, also lead to a stunning viewpoint, pretty lake, rushing stream or lovely waterfalls. In addition, this book includes trails that require little to no travel on gravel/logging roads, to avoid car sickness on bumpy roads.

Because trails outside of parks depend on the enthusiasm of volunteers, you should still be prepared for comparatively rough conditions – but not always. Though wet spots are more common outside parks than in, volunteers have often built bridges and boardwalks or their loggy equivalent. Though bushes (especially salal) sometimes encroach, sometimes they are trimmed well back from the path. While signs are usually absent, sometimes they are inventive and charmingly placed just where they are most welcome. Flagging tape, rope on steep sections, stepping stones, banked trails and even benches all show the enthusiasm of volunteers.

Usually all trail builders share each others' work cheerfully. Sometimes, though, resentment can surface. Mountain bikers can be particularly susceptible to receiving such resentment, it seems, even though many trails that walkers adopt were originally carved out of the bushes by bikers. In fact, that is exactly the case with some of the trail descriptions here. A little gratitude, tolerance and cooperation can go a long way!

Erosion and mud holes result from heavy trail use. That, however, is the case no matter what the form of use. All trail use has an impact on nature. Specific conditions are susceptible to different kinds of impact. Feet, tires and horse hoofs that can be invisible in some circumstances can create havoc in others.

Difficulty

While it is the common practice to designate a trail as simple, moderate or difficult, those terms are not helpful for families with toddlers and teens. What is easy for a teen may be insurmountable for a toddler. In addition, the term "difficult" is itself unclear. A difficult trail may simply be long and tiring, or it may be short and steep, or it may have a section requiring sure-footedness and balance. So this book describes exactly what kind of difficulty you might encounter. The wise parent, therefore, will consider everything. Keeping in mind the ages, temperaments, interests and general physical fitness levels of the children, this wise parent will look at all three kinds of difficulty. A child who has decent endurance but is not sure-footed will be better suited to one kind of a trail than another. The reverse also is the case for a child who will happily leap across a log bridge and dart up a rocky bit of trail but is unlikely to last very long up a long, gentle climb.

When thinking about the length of a hike, you will find not here a whiff of information about the time to allow. When factoring in the toddler vs. teen, the dawdler vs. the eager beaver, the muddy track vs. the boardwalk, and then allowing for additional variations in distractions in the form of photo-ops, wildlife sightings, wading expeditions and so on, such information becomes meaningless. If you don't already have a good idea of the time to allow for your children to make it through X km of trail, then you soon will. Do remember, though, as you increase your planning skills, that each 120 m of uphill is – very roughly – equivalent to 1 km of horizontal walking. In addition, remember that while gradual downhills are at least as fast as horizontal paths, steep downhills can be slower than the uphill climbs, depending, again, on the sure-footedness of the child-trekker. The general advice, therefore? Always allow more time than you think you need!

Preparation

Once the trail has been chosen, next on the agenda is a little preparation.

Safety Issues

Safety, of course, is the single most important consideration. First, it is important to realize there is no such thing as a zero-risk walk or hike. There is no such thing as a zero-risk activity of any sort – including sitting in front of the television. On the other hand, there is little to no disadvantage in being a little over-prepared. Exactly what precautions to take depend on many factors, amongst them your own temperament, the resilience of your family, the season and the remoteness of a trip.

Here, at least, are a few things to think about and take seriously.

Weather and Altitude

None of the trips in this book involves a great change in altitude, but don't be surprised if some of the hilltops are noticeably cooler than their bases. The usual advice about dressing in layers, including something waterproof, wearing tough shoes, bringing hats and sunglasses applies to the longer walks. If there is a single greatest danger, it is probably twisting an ankle in cold, wet weather at a remote location, such as Strathcona Park.

Though hypothermia is remotely possible, hyperthermia/heat stroke needs in some rare circumstances at least a little thinking about – but, of course, you've remembered the plentiful drinking water, sun hats and cool clothing!

Animals, Big and Small

Some trailheads are posted with warnings about bears and/or cougars, some of them indicating recent sightings. While, again, the risks of an aggressive encounter are tiny, they are not zero. Be sensible. In remote locations, it might be a good idea to keep small children close, to make a bit of a hubbub as you go and, possibly, carry pepper spray. Dogs can be magnets for harassed bears and even lead bears back to their owners.

Tiny critters, like mosquitoes, can be a nuisance too, of course. You know the drill!

Wasps can be a significant threat, especially during picnics in late summer. Even when family members have no history of allergic response, the wise parent will carry an antihistamine like Benadryl just in case of a severe reaction.

Personal Health

Don't forget any medications that might be necessary, most likely for asthma or allergic reactions (in addition to insect stings). A basic first-aid kit is a good idea for all but the tamest walks. Children, as all parents know, can be highly inventive when it comes to ways of acquiring skinned knees – amongst other things.

Bits and Pieces

Backpack, binoculars, camera, walking poles.

* * *

You may well already be one step ahead in making these kinds of preparations. If not, you will soon be an expert. Now it's time to look at the weather forecast, pack the snacks, muster the troops and choose the perfect trail!

1. MILLSTONE FALLS

*Well-maintained trails along a beautifully forested ravine
and along the sandstone rapids, falls and fish ladders
of Millstone River in Bowen Park.*

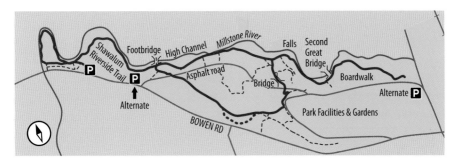

LOCATION
Just south of Pearson Bridge, the prominent landmark on Highway 19A in virtually the centre of Nanaimo, turn up Bowen Road. After about 2.2 km, when you see a playing field on your right, turn into the parking lot.

DISTANCE
3.2-km return; partial loop

ELEVATION GAIN
45 m, cumulative

DIFFICULTY
Easy; one short section by the creek is muddy and rooty in winter, but this section can be bypassed.

SEASON
All year, but winter and spring produce the best water show in the stream. Autumn is good for viewing spawning salmon; summer is best if your children want to venture into some of the park facilities. Choose late April if you love amazing displays of wildflowers.

OF SPECIAL INTEREST FOR CHILDREN

The many rapids and falls are the main reason for visiting the park, but many children will be drawn to the playground and duck pond, both close to the trail.

This old and bizarrely developed city-centre park combines large sections of almost pristine wilderness with intrusive areas of just about every park facility you can think of, from artificial duck ponds with arching bridges to a swimming pool and tennis courts, and from a skate bowl to playing fields. The route recommended here skirts as many of these as possible and generally avoids a paved parkway ploughing through much of the park.

---

1. Head straight ahead (upstream) out of the parking lot, dropping slightly and leaving the asphalt trail for a broad, even, crushed-gravel path. This path keeps gratifyingly close to the stream bank as you walk under many large, old Douglas firs. (To maintain the illusion of wilderness, keep your eyes averted from the houses partly visible across the stream.) The trail curves to your left, and just before the bridge, where the stream emerges from under Bowen Road (and, farther up, Buttertubs Marsh), turns to complete the circuit back to your starting point.

2. Carry on downstream as the paved trail (Shawalum Riverside Trail) first runs away from the stream bank and then approaches it to lead below to another parking lot. Within a few minutes, come to a signposted junction. Although you return along the streamside trail, for your outward trip turn right then immediately left. The trail crosses over a paved road and begins to traverse a forested slope, climbing considerably. A protective chain-link fence runs along this section of the paved trail.

3. When you come to a split, you can take either fork since the trails rejoin in a short distance. Ignoring two more trails leaving almost immediately to your right, keep ahead on the

CLOCKWISE FROM LEFT The rapids slightly above the main falls; the main falls drop in two distinct steps; it is worth leaving the main path to view the upper chute, near the fish ladder.

main trail until visible ahead are a playground, swimming pool and picnic shelter – any or all of which you may wish to visit with your children.

4. Otherwise, turn left downhill and begin a fairly steep descent along a zigzagging trail. In a short distance, when you come to a split, ignore the trail on your right, descending to cross the paved road and, immediately after, an arching stone bridge. The water passing under the bridge and emptying into the duck pond on your right is a side channel of Millstone River. This channel, with its comparatively slow currents that allow spawning salmon to move upstream, can be visited if you wish to explore the next trail on your left before continuing downstream.

5. Drop down the gravel track directly towards the major waterfalls, clearly audible ahead. Falling over horizontal sandstone strata, these stepped falls can be satisfyingly

viewed from many safe angles along the bank. After photographing your fill, return to the riverside trail to carry on downstream, crossing over a little stone bridge and passing a second duck pond, this one with fountains.

6. The trail runs close to the stream from here to a large bridge with a commemorative plaque about the "Second Great Bridge" and an interesting interpretative sign about migrating salmon. You may wish to go to the centre of the bridge for the view, but return to continue downstream. You pass some pretty sections of rapids before coming to two long boardwalks and, beyond them, a large, grassy field with a picnic shelter, and, beyond it, a playground. (Note there are washrooms across the paved road on your right.) This is your turnaround spot.

7. Return the way you came. As you go upstream, appreciate the best viewing angles on the rushing water. When you get to the stepped falls, keep going straight ahead, opting for the small, dirt trail right by the riverbank. If you want to avoid the seasonal mud and roots of this pretty section, you can bypass it since the parallel trail rejoins it a short distance up. The next part of the trail, however, is arguably the prettiest of all: face upstream to take in continually changing views of large firs leaning over the river as it rushes over slabs of sandstone and drops through many small cascades.

8. Turning a little away from the riverbank, the trail crosses over a grated section of the salmon side channel whose downstream end you passed just before the lower falls. Leaving the trail to view the water rushing through a narrow rock chute provides a particularly good view upstream towards a footbridge.

9. Once you arrive at this footbridge, you have reached the junction with your outbound trail. Retrace the short distance back to your vehicle.

2. BUTTERTUBS MARSH

A hidden gem tucked away on the edge of Nanaimo, Buttertubs Marsh Park offers open marsh waters full of water birds, viewing platforms and a beautifully developed loop trail under oaks, arbutus and hawthorns.

LOCATION

From Nanaimo Parkway (Highway 19), turn onto Jingle Pot Road (south), towards Nanaimo city centre (noting that Jingle Pot Road crosses the parkway twice). After 350 m, swing left to stay on Jingle Pot Road, and, almost immediately, take a very sharp left at a curiously unsignposted entrance road to the conservation area's parking lot.

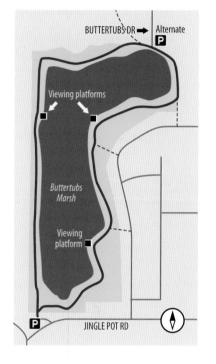

DISTANCE

2.4-km loop

ELEVATION GAIN

Negligible

DIFFICULTY

Supremely easy! Even baby strollers can be spotted making the circuit of level crushed gravel.

SEASON

All season. Of course, the sense of watery expanse is greatest in winter, but even at the end of a hot, dry summer there is plenty of duck-dotted water. When the trees are leafy they provide the best screen against the houses that press up against the east boundary of the area.

OF SPECIAL INTEREST FOR CHILDREN

Preschool children – but only preschool children – are welcome to bring their bicycles. Older children can be primed with some questions and the whole trip turned into a bit of a treasure hunt. What will they discover about the name "Buttertubs"? Canada geese? Ospreys? The amazing Archimedes screw? Then, to top it off (literally), there is the climb to the viewing platform. Binoculars could be fun at this spot.

Leave Fido at home. Dogs are prohibited.

---

1. Walking past the barrier posts, turn right past the large informational sign and map. Stretching before you is a bowerlike view down a long, straight trail. This trail is a raised, dyke-like track through the marsh, with Buttertubs West Marsh (usually with no visible expanse of water) to the left. As you stroll down this track, notice the remarkable presence of Garry oaks and arbutus, remarkable because these gracious trees usually cringe far away from marshes and do not cuddle up right beside them. As you progress past a park bench, observe changing views through gaps in the growth past cattails towards the duck life beyond. The viewing platform is, of course, a must. Don't neglect the particularly restful views towards Mt. Benson over the west marsh.

2. When you reach the north end of the marsh, the trail turns past an unfortunately close residential building before passing an alternate entrance, parking lot and – possibly of great interest at this point – washrooms. (Note that it is only a short walk to Millstone River and park from here.) Turn right to begin the walk along the winding east side of the marsh. Generally, the nearby houses are thoroughly out of sight. One of the most unusual features of this part of the walk is the astounding density of hawthorn, festooned with white blossom in May and thick with red berries for many months following.

CLOCKWISE FROM ABOVE The north side of the marsh looking towards Mt. Benson; the high viewing platform is an excellent spot at which to wield binoculars and cameras; the marsh waters are a magnet for ducks.

The path along the south side in a bower of Garry oak.

3. As you make your winding way back along this bushy shore, you come upon two prominent viewing spots with boardwalk platforms and several interpretative signs.

3. WESTWOOD LAKE

*A surprisingly untouched forest and lake, Westwood Lake
Park and Trail is tucked away at the edges of a hilltop suburb.*

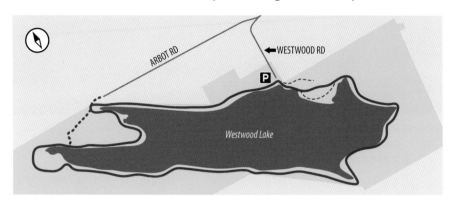

LOCATION
From Highway 19 as it passes Nanaimo, turn west (away from
downtown Nanaimo) at the southern exit onto Jingle Pot Road.
(Jingle Pot Road has two exits.) Drive for 500 m and turn onto
Westwood Road until it comes to its end 1 km along, at West-
wood Lake Park.

DISTANCE
5.5-km loop

ELEVATION GAIN
Negligible

DIFFICULTY
Easy. Almost entirely a broad, gravel path, rising only slightly
over some bluffs at the east end, this is a favourite route for local
joggers as well as walkers.

SEASON
All season

One of the "secret" little beaches off the trail near the south end of the lake.

OF SPECIAL INTEREST FOR CHILDREN

Nanaimo's only lifeguard-protected freshwater swimming hole is right beside the parking area. The circuit of the lake is almost entirely doable for kids on bikes, though the official mountain-biking route is along nearby trails.

1. From the public beach park, turn left, making sure you take the trail closest to the water (the mountain-biking trail to the left swings away from the shore considerably). As you leave the crowds behind and enter the forest of large Douglas fir, you come to an area of bluffs where user-made trails branch off into a bit of a network. Some of these lead to small, hidden beaches, others to rounded, rocky bluffs.

2. Keeping to, or returning to the main trail, you reach the end of the lake and some lovely views up the length of the lake. Even stumps and dead spars rising out of the water make for striking images. Pass by some large cedars, go over a small bridge and boardwalks and come to a tiny inlet with pretty views from a rounded rock bluff. Ignore trails leading to your left, which connect to Morrell Lake.

3. Passing around the end of this little inlet, you are faced with a choice of trails. The off-leash trail for bounding pooches is by far the less attractive alternative, running as it does

The northwest end of the lake is a fascinating tangle of logs and vegetation.

under power lines parallel to the lakeshore. Taking the lakeside trail, you feel immersed in a forest of large fir and cedar. If you choose the path following the shore, you pass over boardwalks and Westwood Stream rushing towards the lake.

4. Reaching the northwest end of the lake and the northern junction with the off-leash trail, the trail dips to the right, crossing another bridge and taking you to the head of a little inlet with some striking images of logs, stumps and water lilies. When you are given the option of taking the shortcut trail, unless you are tired, opt for Lake Trail. Rounding the peninsula takes you over more boardwalks and to the head of the next inlet.

5. Side trails join from the left, but always keep to the right and the signposted Lake Trail. Although the trail here is immediately below a suburb, trees and the bank largely protect your eyes – and your nature-craving soul. Via more sections of boardwalk, you are soon back to the two beaches and main parking area.

4. MORRELL NATURE SANCTUARY

A maze of trails leading to a rocky knoll of manzanita and arbutus, a viewing platform over Beaver Pond, and a lakeside route amongst cedars.

LOCATION
From the Nanaimo Parkway (Highway 19), turn east (towards downtown Nanaimo) at the traffic lights sign-posted for Fifth Street and Vancouver Island University. Drive 800 m, turn right onto Wakesiah Avenue and proceed for 270 m. At Nanaimo Lakes Road, turn right and drive 1.2 km, until you see the sign for Morrell Nature Sanctuary on your right.

DISTANCE
4 km

ELEVATION GAIN
75 m

DIFFICULTY
Easy level paths most of the way. The side route to the top of a rocky knoll and viewpoint is a little rougher. At one or two spots, newly fallen arbutus leaves in July can be slippery.

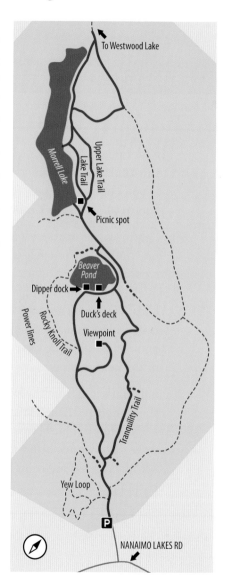

To Westwood Lake

Morrell Lake

Upper Lake Trail

Lake Trail

Picnic spot

Beaver Pond

Dipper dock

Duck's deck

Viewpoint

Power lines

Rocky Knoll Trail

Tranquility Trail

Yew Loop

NANAIMO LAKES RD

SEASON
All season, but there a few slightly wet spots in winter. Beaver Pond can be nearly dry at the end of a long, dry summer.

OF SPECIAL INTEREST FOR CHILDREN
The most distinctive features of the route include the high viewpoint, so-called Beaver Pond, and Morrell Lake itself. All should appeal to different facets of your child's personality. The lake isn't brilliant for swimming, but it does have a little beach and a picnic area (with washrooms), so there is plenty of opportunity for getting up to no good.

1. Walk straight ahead from the parking lot, passing the administrative office, side trails to wheelchair-accessible routes and, later, Tranquility Trail. Pass through the gate appealingly signed for Rocky Knoll Trail. Ignore a second sign for Tranquility, and soldier on through sword ferns and cedars, some of them large and buttressed with enthusiastically writhing roots. If you have the right kind of child, do take time to pause at the interpretative signs for Indian pipe and western coral root, both about as weird and wonderful as local flora get.

2. As the trail rises through a drier and rockier area, notice other signs, most notably for the comparatively rare hairy manzanita, a truly wonderful kind of miniature arbutus. Pass a picnic table and climb some dirt-and-timber stairs until you come to an unlabelled fork in the trail.

3. Not on most maps of the park, the side trail to the right leads to arguably the loveliest spot in the park, though it is a dead-end trail requiring you to return to this spot. Take a deep breath and begin the ascent over largely bare rock, through arbutus and – bonus! – lots of manzanita bushes. The park bench perched on the perfect viewpoint makes both a good rest spot and good turnaround point.

4. Return to Rocky Knoll Trail, turn right and within a few steps, find yourself with two branches both leading along

FROM LEFT An unusual view of Mt. Benson from the side trail to the viewpoint; the northwest end of Morrell Lake.

Beaver Pond Loop. Take the trail to the right and, within mere minutes, come to a sturdily built boardwalk leading you to Dipper Dock and a viewpoint for a pond, Duck's Deck, and the wildlife it contains. Unfortunately, it is unlikely to contain any wildlife if you arrive at the end of a dry summer, when not a trace of water is to be found.

5. Returning to the trail, turn left to follow the shore of the pond. Note the side trails. Take the third of these through a gate leading a short distance to a service road and turn left. If you see an "11" on a post on Beaver Pond Trail, you've gone too far; turn back to find the short route to the service road. A few steps along the service road brings you within sight of the clearing by Morrell Lake.

6. The little beach isn't quite Copacabana, but children can be easy to please as long as there is water to hand. After using the beach, picnic table or outhouses, carry on around Morrell Lake. At a few points there are very pretty views, though prettier looking along the lake rather than across it, unless you have a morbid interest in power lines. Notice the two trails leading away from the lake, since you use them on your return route.

7. Be careful – the trails at the end of the lake are configured differently from what maps typically show. Once at the end of the lake, take the trail leading directly away from the lake and come to a T junction with a broad trail (leading, if you were to turn left, towards Westwood Lake). Turn right, climbing gradually along a broad, gravelly trail under alders.

8. Before long, on your right, notice the brown gate and sign for Lake Trail (called "Connector" on some maps). Turn down this trail until you get to the lake. Turn left to repeat a short distance along the lakeside trail before turning left onto Upper Lake Trail to loop back to the head of the lake and the service road. This trail rises slightly and drops down some dirt-and-timber stairs. Although it is well away from the lake, you can see the lake through the bare trunks of second-growth Douglas fir.

9. Now that you're back on the service road, carry on past the first trail to Beaver Pond, and take the second one. This will allow you to make the short connection at Beaver Pond to Tranquility Trail, your route back to the beginning. This trail, so named, it seems, because it has no distinctive visible features, rolls purposefully along through blankets of salal and large trees, roughly parallel to the rocky knoll, rising on your right. Ignore Lookout Trail on your left (unless you want to make a short return trip) and carry on to a fork. Here you can turn either right or left. Both directions will deliver you after a short distance to your starting point.

5. COLLIERY DAM PARK

Historically interesting dammed lakes, good for swimming and fishing, and a varied walk amongst venerable cedars and firs. More than 100 years ago, the dams were built as a water source for washing coal and mine mules, then for domestic use by locals.

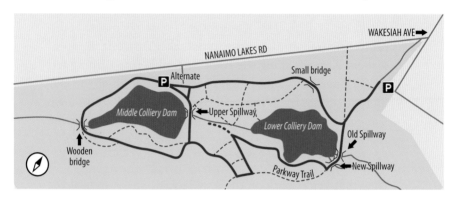

LOCATION
From the Nanaimo Parkway (Highway 19), turn towards Nanaimo at the Fifth Street intersection (by Vancouver Island University). After 1.2 km, make a right turn onto Wakesiah Avenue. Drive just under 0.6 km to the signposted park entrance.

DISTANCE
2-km loop

ELEVATION GAIN
45 m

DIFFICULTY
Easy, broad paths, mostly of level, much-used bark mulch, with a few paved sections.

SEASON

All season, but winter is best for viewing the foaming frenzy of the slipways. Summer is, unsurprisingly, best for taking advantage of the swimming holes.

OF SPECIAL INTEREST FOR CHILDREN

Not just one, but two small swimming lakes – and, if the water is too cool for a dip and you come prepared, the two lakes double as fishing holes. Crossing slipways and bridges and climbing up to giant boulders give lots of variety to the walk.

1. Passing the washrooms, turn into the forest while keeping the lower lake on your left. A Harewood History sign is just possibly more interesting for its photos than its information about this part of Nanaimo, but worth a pause. Cross over a bridge beside slightly eerie concrete industrial relics and come to another informational sign, this one, perhaps ironically, about invasive plants.

2. Ignore a trail on the left to carry on up the major trail past some maples, (invasive!) holly trees and English ivy towards a second parking lot and picnic spot. If you happen to have poochykins with you, you can let her off leash for the second part of this figure-eight circuit. Turn left to cross over the upper spillway. In winter, at least, you can enjoy the foam and fury of the rushing water before reaching the far shore and a photo-worthy view of the upper lake and its three little swimming spots.

3. Turn right to circumnavigate the upper lake, but, instead of clinging to the lakeshore, climb up towards some huge slabs of higgledy-piggledy sandstone. Set amongst ferns and cedars, encrusted with moss, these sandstone formations are well worth the price of admission.

4. Once past the boulders, ignore the trail leading straight ahead, and instead turn down the slope back towards the lake. Within minutes, come to a set of concrete steps (with

CLOCKWISE FROM LEFT After winter rains, the flow from the upper lake; leave the trail to visit this fantasyscape of giant, mossy boulders; the calm waters of the lake are used for swimming and fishing.

no handrail) leading to a wonderfully picturesque wooden bridge. Cross the zigzagging bridge above the stream in the gorge and turn right.

5. This road-width, broad path leads back to the parking lot you passed earlier. If you didn't properly enjoy the spillway the first time, here is your second chance. Cross again, but this time turn left when you come to a paved path (part of Parkway Trail.) Descending this path, come to a red fire hydrant on your left. Turning left onto the mulch path allows you to head upstream a little to a good viewing spot of the water rushing out of the spillway.

The impressively engineered walkway and bridge at the south end of the loop.

6. Carry on past the lower lake, and cross over a new spillway, built amidst much controversy about whether to drain the lakes or how best to prevent disaster should the weakening old spillway (farther along) give way. Within minutes you are past the lower lake and back to your car (possibly via the washrooms).

6. RICHARDS MARSH PARK

A little-known marsh with a long, beautifully built boardwalk and fascinating interpretative posters.

LOCATION

From Highway 19, south of Nanaimo, take the turn towards Nanaimo onto Highway 1 and drive for just under 500 m. If you're approaching from Highway 1, look for South Gate Mall in Chase River. Extension Road is about 200 m south. Turn onto Extension Road and drive 1.2 km to Rajeena Way. Turn left and drive 500 m to the end of the road. Parking isn't great here, but there are spots along the curb.

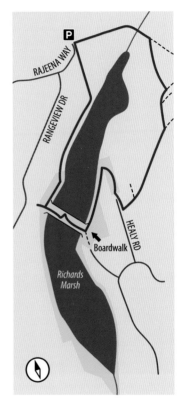

DISTANCE

2-km loop (1.2-km return without loop)

ELEVATION GAIN

30 m

DIFFICULTY

Easy, partly on groomed trails and boardwalk. The optional loop section is a dirt track that can get a little muddy in winter.

SEASON

All season. The water level in the marsh, of course, varies depending on how hot and dry the season has been, but an open body of water near the north end of the marsh (a great collecting spot for ducks and other water birds) remains throughout the year.

Much of the marsh is cattails and other marsh vegetation.

OF SPECIAL INTEREST FOR CHILDREN

The long, snaking boardwalk suspended over the marsh and the colourfully illustrated signs should have an otherworldly fascination for most kids. The gauntlet of blackberry bushes towards the end of summer can be a tasty diversion.

1. From the concrete barriers at the end of the road you see two tracks: one to the left and one to the right. If you elect to do the full loop walk, your return track is on your left. At this point, though, turn right to walk behind a few houses towards the edge of the marsh. The first part of the marsh-side trail runs closest to the permanently open-water area, so take the time to peer through the trees at whatever mergansers or Virginia rails that happen to be visiting.

2. Pass a park boundary sign and, as the trail reaches a T junction, turn left to explore the most fascinating part of the park – the boardwalk. The views up and down the long, narrow marshlands, with foreground cattails and background forest and mountains, are unusual and striking. When the trees are in leaf, you may not be aware of the bevies of houses screened by the trees.

FROM LEFT The boardwalk gives a wonderful sense of being immersed in the marsh environment; a view of the marsh and Mt. Benson from the north end.

3. Cross to the end of the boardwalk and turn left to follow the east shore of the marsh. The next section of the loop is not through park but follows old tracks, primarily used by locals. You may, therefore, prefer to retrace your route rather than undertake the whole loop. The end of this trail can sometimes be under siege by invasive Himalayan blackberry bushes. Reaching the end of the trail, turn up the track to climb towards a cul-de-sac and a subdivision.

4. Before the nature-loving side of your personality is quite squashed, you can leave the subdivision behind. After passing four or five houses, pick out a bare dirt track on the left of the road winding into the alders. Follow this broad track through the small trees as it tends gradually downhill, roughly parallel to the (invisible) edge of the marsh. Ignore one small track to the left near the beginning. As you approach a significant turn to the left, pass another track to the right and, at the corner to begin your descent, two more.

5. Reaching the level of the marsh, cross a little bridge and pass yet another track leading to the right before climbing slightly to reach a kind of crossroads. A sharp left takes you a short distance back to your car.

7. MORDEN COLLIERY

A well-groomed trail running past historic colliery ruins, beneath some giant cottonwoods, to the forested bank of the Nanaimo River. The first part of the trail leads through Morden Colliery Historic Provincial Park, but the trail thereafter is built by volunteers and listed as a regional district trail.

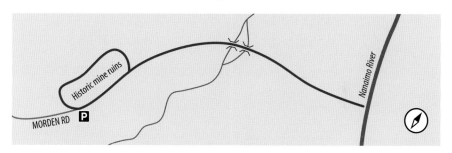

LOCATION
The park is well-signposted from Highway 1, about 2 km south of the Duke Point Ferry Terminal. If you are travelling south, turn left onto Morden Road and simply drive straight ahead to the park entrance, about 1 km along.

DISTANCE
2.4-km return

ELEVATION GAIN
Negligible

DIFFICULTY
Extremely easy. The trail of mostly crushed gravel is level, smooth and well-maintained.

SEASON
All season

FROM LEFT The double bridges near the south end of the trail; one of the historical coal-mining structures near the beginning of the trail.

OF SPECIAL INTEREST FOR CHILDREN

The concrete ruins of bits and pieces of the colliery are sufficiently strange and picturesque to capture the imagination, especially when aided by informational signs. For nature-minded children who like a treasure hunt, there is a large illustrated sign describing plants and flowers in the park. For children who love their bikes and are unenthused by walking, the trail is possible for tyke-bikes that can handle a gravel surface.

1. Turn right out of the parking lot to follow the attractively winding gravel trail. One sign points out that the trail follows the route of a former coal railway; another illustrates wildflowers and plants along the trail. Passing initially through alders, you soon see many large cedars and on your right, just before a bend in the trail, a huge cottonwood.

The trail ends with views of the Nanaimo River.

2. The trail crosses two pretty bridges in succession beneath the shade of some large alders and through thickets of salmonberries. The next section of trail is best for viewing large cottonwoods, though an impressive maple rises on the left too.

3. The trail ends at a steep but low bank of the Nanaimo River. It is possible to scramble down a dirt slope to the river, which, of course, is exactly what many children will feel driven to do. The views in both directions up and down the slow-moving river are idyllic.

4. Returning the way you came, arrive at a right fork in the trail as you approach the colliery ruins. Turn right to follow a semi-circular trail amongst the ruins and back to your car.

8. NANAIMO RIVER

Easy access to the crystalline, pleasant and quiet pools of the Nanaimo River, flowing past low gravel banks overhung with large trees.

LOCATION

Follow the signs on Highway 1 for the turn-off to Morden Colliery Historic Provincial Park, which is well-signposted from Highway 1, about 2 km south of the Duke Point Ferry Terminal.

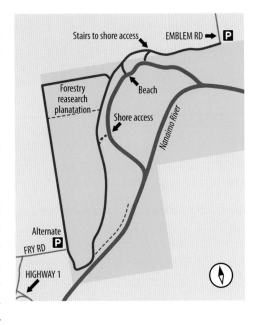

If you are travelling south, turn left onto Morden Road and simply drive straight ahead. Instead of proceeding to the park, though, turn right almost immediately onto Main Road, signposted for Nanaimo River Regional Park. Continue straight ahead onto Thatcher Road for almost 2 km. Turn right at the sign for the park and drive 300 m to the end of the road.

DISTANCE

2.8-km partial loop

ELEVATION GAIN

Negligible

DIFFICULTY

Easy, broad, level path. A few sturdy stairs with a handrail.

SEASON

All season. Warm weather is best for water play, of course, but children can be eye-poppingly able to take pleasure in water at the most peculiar times of year.

OF SPECIAL INTEREST FOR CHILDREN

Water. Calm, easily accessible water. Lots of water. And bikes. In fact, the park encourages bicycles, especially those that will handle dirt or gravel.

1. No sooner do you start along the trail than you see a sturdy little flight of wooden stairs leading to the riverbank. Just beyond a few scattered trees, come to a curious shore of sandstone plates. Immediately below, the water is still, deep enough to be serious and crystal clear (except in winter floods). Walk along the sandstone to experience the bumps and slabs of this weird and wonderful shoreline.

2. Return to the bank-top trail via the wooden stairs and turn left to follow the river upstream. Pass a pretty, split-cedar fence and a yellow sign warning of the eroding bank. No doubt members of your troop will point out that the fine gravel beach at the base of the banks is a perfect splashing spot. As you head farther upstream, through small alders and maples, notice the path is now more or less atop a dyke – though the trail is no longer alongside the main channel of the river.

3. When you come to a set of timber-and-gravel steps, see a blue and white sign indicating that the river trail is both straight ahead and to the right. Turn right to take the steps. (You might have to lug a child's bicycle down this bit.) Pass through a research plantation before coming across another signpost indicating a sharp turn to the left.

4. At this point the trail is a slightly dull, straight-as-a-die service road. When you come to another sign, indicating the river trail goes both left and straight ahead, continue

FROM LEFT Flat slabs of sandstone make wading and splashing an unusual experience at this access spot; the crystal-clear water of the river when the water level is low.

straight ahead. The trail to the left is a kind of shortcut (though it doesn't appear on the official park trail map). Carry on past informative signs about forest research, past an alternate park entrance, almost to the river. It is worthwhile reading the information poster here, particularly for what it says about salmon in the river and endangered Douglas fir ecosystems.

5. Hesitate before descending onto the rough trail by the riverbank and running along the shore. This trail becomes increasingly uneven and bushy before petering out. Instead, keep on the dyke-top trail. When you come to some timber-and-gravel steps leading to the right, you may wish to go down them to find your way to a gravel beach along the backwaters of the main river. Return to the dyke-top trail, turn right and find your way back to the beginning.

9. HEMER PARK

A long, easy loop trail through large cedars and along the shores of two different lakes in Hemer Provincial Park.

LOCATION

If you're approaching from the north, on Highway 1, turn onto Cedar Road by the intersection of Highways 1 and 19. Drive for 5 km along Cedar Road until you come to Hemer Road, on your left. Hemer Park is 1.5 km along Hemer Road.

If you're approaching from the south, pass Nanaimo Airport and turn right onto Haslam Road. Continue to the end of Haslam, 3 km along, where it forms a T junction with Cedar Road. Turn left and continue along Cedar Road until it swings left. After 2.3 km, turn right onto Woodbank Road and drive 650 m. Turn right onto Hemer Road and drive to its end, 750 m along.

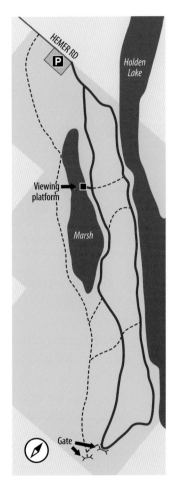

DISTANCE

3.4-km loop (with more possible)

ELEVATION GAIN

Negligible

DIFFICULTY

Broad, groomed dirt paths with only occasional roots or slight dips.

SEASON

All season

CLOCKWISE FROM LEFT Waterlilies and cedars on the marsh near Holden Lake; the long marsh from the viewing platform; the main trail runs along the shores of Holden Lake.

OF SPECIAL INTEREST FOR CHILDREN

A viewing platform with colourful interpretative signs can (with the right children) be a great place to hunker down for a lot of pointing and exclaiming at ducks, ducks and more ducks. In addition, though the trails are not designated as cycling trails, children who are more motivated by two wheels than by two feet could, unobtrusively, pedal earnestly alongside watchful parents. Neither the unnamed marshy lake nor the much larger and deeper Holden Lake is good for swimming, alas.

1. For the most attractive of several possible routes, walk past the parking area at the end of the marshy lake on your right. Although this appears on the park map as a green area, with no open water, in fact, this very pretty – but marshy – lake has lots of open water, and, of course, the ducky life to go with it. Notice the potentially useful outhouse just off the

trail to the left. Keep to this trail with the water on your right, ignoring cross trails leading off to the left.

2. When you come to a viewing platform off the main trail, do take the time to visit it for lovely views of the water-lily and cattail embellished waters. Returning to the main trail, continue to the end of the marshy lake. Here the main trail swings a little to the left and then right, to follow the course of a small creek. Two more trails branch to the left, but all trails converge at the south end of the park.

3. Here life gets a little confusing, not just because you must pass through a gate for a few metres before swinging left and heading towards Holden Lake but also because there are clearly some recent issues with property lines here – though they may be tidied up by the time you visit. At this writing, large, red metal fences have been erected, along with unwelcoming signs. However, the enthusiasm of trail walkers has led to the forging of a clear route skirting these alarming-looking fences and leading to the shores of the lake. Here, passing through a yellow gate, you are once again safe in the embrace of the provincial park.

4. Continue along the shore of the lake, pausing at gaps in the small bushes to gain the best views. Towards the north end of the trail, the path passes a bench, branches off in trails to the left and crosses over a little metal bridge. When you come to a sign for Morden Colliery Provincial Park, allow yourself to be a little puzzled if you have visited that park. In fact, this trail currently leads only *towards* the colliery, not actually to it, and it won't until/unless a bridge is built over the Nanaimo River.

5. Swing left to rise into the woods and cross the short distance to the beginning of the trail.

6. If you want to do more exploring, there are many more trails in the area, many of them used by horses.

10. YELLOW POINT PARK &
YELLOW POINT BOG ECOLOGICAL RESERVE

*Showcases a spectacular camas lily display in late spring
and a complex network of trails, partly through fir forest,
partly running past small lakes and along the tops
of mossy sandstone ridges.*

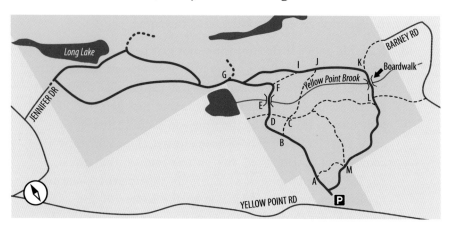

LOCATION
Approximately 6 km north of Ladysmith, turn north onto Cedar
Road. Drive 3 km and turn right onto Yellow Point Road. After
slightly more than 4 km, look for the large sign for Yellow Point
Park on your left.

DISTANCE
4.8 km, largely a double loop (shorter loops also well-signposted)

ELEVATION GAIN
60 m, cumulative, over rolling land

DIFFICULTY
Generally, very easy, except some very muddy spots in winter.

SEASON

April is the absolute highlight for the astounding display of wild camas. The rest of the year is good too (except, of course, for the muddy spots in winter).

OF SPECIAL INTEREST FOR CHILDREN

The meticulous (and clever) way in which each of the many junctions is signposted with a letter means that children might enjoy scampering ahead to the next letter sign to wait for their trudging parents. For this route, that sequence is A, B, D, E, F, G, H. After the (unsignposted) loop through the ecological reserve, the sequence picks up from H, to G, I, J, K, L and M.

1. If you're visiting in the latter part of April, you'll want to linger in the camas fields. Glance meaningfully at (or put to good use) the picnic tables and outhouse, and head left to begin a clockwise sortie. Enter a forest largely of fir and salal. The trail rises a little over some slightly exposed sandstone and then makes a slight descent. In fact, the whole park (all Yellow Point, much of Nanaimo and most of the southern Gulf Islands) is composed of ridges of sandstone running northwest–southeast. During this trip, find yourself walking along nearly level moss-covered, rounded shoals of sandstone or dropping down into the low spots between ridges.

2. When you come to a sign with the letter B, and the words "You Are Here," stop both to admire the planning that virtually eliminates the chances of becoming disoriented and to take a visual fix on the kind of signs to look for at many points. Fork left to drop down a ridge, and cross an occasionally wet area, to come to crossroads D. Going straight ahead, descend even more towards Yellow Point Brook (not much of a brook even at the wettest of times). Pause at the majestic fir on your right for a little hugging. The so-called Horse Crossing, removed for replacement, may still be missing when you arrive, so you may have to wobble your way across the brook on a few improvised planks.

CLOCKWISE FROM TOP Clouds of camas near the beginning of the trail; late April and early May are generally the season for the camas bloom; Long Lake glimpsed from the trail through the ecological reserve.

3. Climbing slightly to the fork, F, read the information sign for the ecological reserve ahead and turn left to take the mossy-ridge trail first to G, then H. At H, fork left and descend through small firs towards a little lake visible through the trees. Pass a sign for Jennifer Road and persevere parallel to the lakeshore through (or around) some spots that become ridiculously muddy during wet weather. Once across the seasonal mud, head left towards the comparatively narrow trail running immediately next to a fence. A side trail loops off this fence trail but rejoins at the top of the rise beyond the lake.

4. Arriving at a white gate in the fence to the left, breathe a sigh of relief as a broad and smooth trail opens out to your right. Although this trail narrows, it runs nearly straight along the mossy ridge. When you arrive at a T junction at the bottom of a dip, you may spot a broken signpost saying "Yellow Point." A few steps up the trail to the left lies a public road. For your onward route, therefore, turn right. A short distance along, come to another fork and signpost for Yellow Point Park, pointing right.

5. Follow the subsequent traversing trail, running parallel to and slightly above Long Lake (a lake name much used all over Vancouver Island). At the end of the lake the trail drops and wanders through a seasonally squelchy area and climbs to a T junction. Turn right to join a trail, usually with lots of evidence of horse traffic, which continues to climb before passing over a ridge. (This well-used trail doesn't appear on the posted maps in the area.) From the top of the ridge, drop and rise to the next ridge before swinging left. Within minutes you have completed the loop back to the first lake.

6. Retrace the trail by the fence until you come to sign H, back in the park. Take the right fork, towards G. Once again in new territory, take the left fork towards I, passing signpost J (towards Barney Road) and ignoring the trail signposted "Fern Gully Bridge." Between J and K, enjoy a section of ridgetop mossy trail. At K, turn right towards L, crossing a sturdy boardwalk bridge and climbing significantly through thickets of salal before contouring along your last section of ridgetop mossy trail.

7. Once you are at L, the increasingly broad trail leads you more or less directly to M and across the camas meadows to the parking lot. Remember the outhouse and picnic table? If they weren't useful before, they may well be now!

The signposted "Big Tree" next to the trail.

11. CHRISTIE FALLS

A combination of the Trans Canada (TCT)/Cowichan Valley Trail and a side trail to a spectacular sequence of falls, each with its own character.

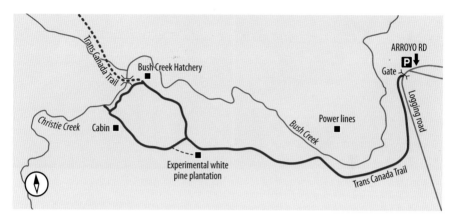

LOCATION

On the northern outskirts of Ladysmith at a significant exit, turn onto Grouhel Road. Drive 200 m and turn right onto Christie Road for 1.7 km. Turn left onto Arroyo Road and drive a short distance to a gate where there is a barrage of dire warning signs about the logging roads ahead. Fear not. The trailhead from the logging road, where most visitors park, is about 150 m ahead at another gate on the right. Since, however, signs warn that the first gate may be locked at any time, you might feel most comfortable parking alongside the road outside this gate and hoofing it the short stretch to the TCT branch.

DISTANCE

6.8 km

ELEVATION GAIN

125 m

FROM LEFT The lowest in the sequence of falls; the apron falls partway up the creek-side trail.

DIFFICULTY

Most of the route is along a deactivated logging road now designated as part of the TCT. The trail along Christie Creek to the falls is a narrow dirt track that climbs steadily over rocks and roots, but it requires nothing more than a little sure-footedness and a healthy pair of lungs. There is a narrow, single-log bridge on which you can view one set of falls, but this is an optional extra, not recommended for most children.

SEASON

All season, but obviously the wet season produces the most splash and dash in falls that can dwindle to very little after a long, hot summer.

OF SPECIAL INTEREST FOR CHILDREN

As with so many waterfall trails, this one leads to a highlight that most kids should find exciting, not least of all because there are several different chunks of the many-stepped falls to explore – and many accessible viewpoints from which to see them.

FROM LEFT Interesting double falls converging into a single chute; the uppermost falls drop in a bridal-veil spray.

1. If you have parked outside the first gate by the battery of threatening signs, walk to the Trans Canada Trail sign and the red/orange gate on the right. Pass the gate and continue your traverse up the side of a valley, crossing a culvert and passing under power lines. As you enter a grove of larger trees, you begin probably the most attractive part of the walk up the valley. Here you have something of the impression of being partway to the canopy of the comparatively big hemlock, fir and cedar above a bed of sword ferns far below. For a while you can hear the rush of the creek below you, but you soon leave it behind.

2. As you approach a stand of dense, uniform pine on your left, keep an eye open for a small track. It is worthwhile taking the few steps up this track where you see a sign explaining a research project involving the attempts to develop disease-resistant white pine. Back on the TCT, you soon see a left fork in the road with a sign indicating that the hatchery is on the

larger roadway straight ahead. Note the spot because you return from the falls along the smaller road on the left.

3. The forest opens a little as you pass through smaller trees, and before long you arrive at a large, solid building and a sign about the Bush Creek Hatchery. Another sign gives an aerial-photo view of Christie Falls and the trails. In case you have trouble interpreting this map, note that you have been walking along the broad, green trail to this point, but now will be leaving it to turn left onto the smaller orange trail.

4. Begin the watery part of your tour by making a short detour to the middle of the bridge along the TCT. Return to cross the large open area to admire the first bits of cascade (and possibly take advantage of the outhouse). Start up the signed narrow dirt trail heading up through the trees to the left of the stream. Upstream, pass one particularly grand old fir and some reasonably secure viewpoints over a lovely, fan-shaped cascade.

5. The climax of the falls, though, is a zigzagging sequence of multiple falls cutting around a kind of island. With a family, you are best off appreciating the good views from this side of the creek. At the top of this sequence is a side trail to probably the most impressive falls, shooting out from a crest of rock high above you. However, there is a narrow log bridge (with reasonably good grip and a rope support) to the island and a view of another good bit of waterfall. Don't feel, however, that you're missing out on the best by staying high and dry! You're not.

6. Continue on the signposted trail as it climbs away from the creek, passing a self-consciously cute log cabin, and begin the descent to complete the loop. One short section at the bottom of the descent can be very wet in winter, but thereafter the trail becomes an old roadbed. This curves gradually left (ignore a slightly smaller track to the right) before bringing you back to the junction with the outward route.

12. CHEMAINUS LAKE

*A pretty, little, nearly circular fish-stocked lake, bounded
by municipal forest, circled by an easy, well-designed path.*

LOCATION
This is one of those little gems
hidden in plain sight. On Highway 1, 1.5 km north of the traffic lights and main turnoff to
Chemainus Road (Henry Road),
turn west onto River Road. Just
0.5 km along, turn right at the
signposted entrance to the park.

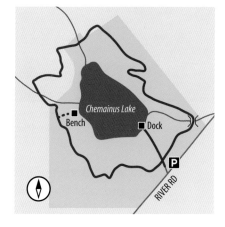

DISTANCE
2.8 km

ELEVATION GAIN
20 m, cumulative

DIFFICULTY
Easy, level path nearly all the way.

SEASON
All season, but spring and fall are best for fishing (stocks drop
during warm summer months).

OF SPECIAL INTEREST FOR CHILDREN
Fishing is permitted from the little dock at the south end. In
fact, the lake is stocked with catchable-sized rainbow trout.
With or without fishing tackle, this dock and the picnic table on
the east shore make perfect munchfest spots, one in full sun,
the other in shade. It is possible for adept children, who hate
walking but like biking, to ride most of the trail while the rest of
the family walks.

CLOCKWISE FROM LEFT Lily pads and other shallow-water plants are amongst the lake's attractions; the view south across the lake from the fishing float; most of the lake is bordered by reed beds.

1. Turn right from the parking lot, passing the information sign, and take the broad, groomed, crushed-gravel trail to cross a sturdy little Billy Goat Gruff bridge. This first part of the trail winds prettily by some large firs and cedars, in a bed of sword ferns.

2. The trail passes a picnic table, takes a sharp turn to swing well away from the lake and rises to join a road-width dirt section of trail, all the while skirting the marshlands that border the lake nearly all the way around. Occasionally, however, views across the lake and its usually calm, reflective surface make for contented sighs.

3. As the trail drops and passes the north end of the lake, notice from an attractive viewpoint that you can see the little dock immediately opposite. This marks, roughly, the halfway spot.

4. Alternating between gravel and dirt sections, the last section of trail is generally well above and back from the lake, gently rising and dropping.

5. Returning to your starting spot, turn left to visit the little fishing dock. If you have an avid angler in the family, this is obviously a good time to pick up all the fishing paraphernalia you need from the familymobile.

13. CHEMAINUS RIVER

A series of loop trails along a forested river remarkable for its deep, largely still pools, by small gravel beaches or sculpted rock bluffs. This trail runs through Chemainus River Provincial Park, but as is the case with many provincial parks, this one is undeveloped.

LOCATION
On Highway 1, between Chemainus and Duncan, at the traffic lights, turn onto Highway 18 signposted for Cowichan Lake. At just under 7 km, turn right onto Hillcrest Road (a gravel logging road). After 6 km, come to a small gravel parking area on the right, with a bit of a concrete barrier and a sign on a tree forbidding the use of motorized vehicles on the trails.

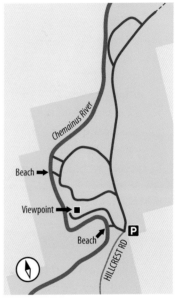

DISTANCE
3-km series of loops

ELEVATION GAIN
20 m, cumulative, over an essentially flat area with trails down to and up from the riverbank.

DIFFICULTY
Easy, broad trails (many ATV tracks).

SEASON
Year-round, but swimmers clearly will zero in on summer.

OF SPECIAL INTEREST FOR CHILDREN
Splashing, wading, swimming, cavorting...the appeal of the park is obvious.

FROM ABOVE A beautiful large cedar overhangs a deep pool downstream from the park entrance; the view into the deep pool from the bluffs.

1. The first of the four down-and-up trails to the river is by far the shortest, and the prettiest. Simply cross the dirt road and walk a short distance until you see a broad (ATV-width) track leading down the slope and onto a gravel bar. At a sharp S curve in the Chemainus River, a gravel bar serves as a great beach with easy access to deep, jade-green pools of luscious, clear water. Last one in…!

2. Returning up the slope, come to a bare area under firs. Keep to the left, roughly parallel to the curve in the river, and take another broad track down towards the river. En route, have a fine bank-top view of the beach you just left and be treated to a chainsaw carving that makes up in fun what it may lack in subtle skill. This dead-end track leads down behind a log jam and only awkward access to the river.

3. Back at the top of the slope, turn left along the gravel logging road. After a few minutes, notice a sign high on a fir to the left of the road, announcing this to be Chemainus River Park and telling you what you mustn't do. Here you see the beginning of the third approach to the river, another broad track curving in a large loop through salal and under firs.

4. A steady tromp will bring you to the level of the river, and a short side track to the river with a small rocky beach overhung by a grand old maple. Return the short distance on this loop route, and a short walk later take the next side trail to the riverside. Here you find a short, fairly steep drop by a large cedar to view a gravel bar and a very wee set of proto-rapids. Return to the loop track to make your way back up a substantial slope towards the gravel road.

5. To reach the last loop off the gravel road, you need to undertake a substantial trek of several hundred metres. Pass a yellow sign saying "3 Km UP" (don't worry – this makes sense to logging vehicles). Just a few metres afterwards, take the fork to the left and almost immediately see the riverbank ahead at the bottom of the slope. This is probably not the

The favoured swimming spot near the first access to the river.

spot you want to seek out if you have getting wet on your agenda. The track stops in a clearing at the top of a steep little bank. Though there are trails down this bank, they do lead to a large boulder floodplain, with the river itself still a good distance away.

6. Carry on past this viewpoint to complete the loop by climbing a steep little slope back up to the gravel road. If you really are determined to get some exercise and do a little exploring, you can turn left and go farther along this logging road, since, for the most part, it is free of traffic. The accessible part of the river exploration is complete, however, so most intrepid hikers will simply want to stroll along the road back to the patiently waiting car.

14. ROTARY MCADAM PARK

Broad, easy trails alongside the Cowichan River near downtown Duncan, under large cottonwoods and featuring several viewing platforms with colourful and informative signs.

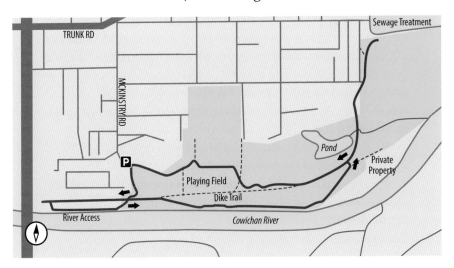

LOCATION

After crossing the silver bridge towards the centre of Duncan, if you are heading north, turn right at the first set of traffic lights, onto Trunk Road. When you come to a second traffic-light intersection, turn right again, onto McKinstry Road, and follow it more or less to its end. Park in the large lot on the left, beside tennis courts.

DISTANCE

About 3 km, depending on some choices.

ELEVATION GAIN

Negligible

DIFFICULTY

In spite of some signs warning of a potentially "uneven surface", the trails are broad, level and generally well groomed, in most places suitable even for wheely walkers.

SEASON

All year, but a hot summer's day will obviously bring out the strongest interest in the water. Late August through September can be good times to spot chinook/spring salmon (those are the big ones, number one on the orca menu!). They will be heading upstream to spawn, and may be comparatively easy to spot, as their numbers have increased in the Cowichan River in some recent years. Winter floods can make for some dramatic views of swirling water.

OF SPECIAL INTEREST FOR CHILDREN

While the water might be the main interest, the spawning salmon, and the blackberry bushes (mid-August to September), may well spark interest. Those kids who love pedalling on two (or three) wheels rather than walking sedately will be pleased with these trails. Many children will also like the viewing platforms with beautifully illustrated and informative signs about local heritage and animal life. As well, and unique amongst trails in this book, this route will be hugely fascinating for most poo-fix-ated children for the astounding reason that one of the trails allows a strangely educational perspective on sewage treatment ponds!

1. Pass by the tennis courts to the right and head towards the clearly visible gravel ramp leading up to the dike running parallel to the river. Once on the dike, pause at the first set of information signs and, thus enlightened, head to the right along this dike-top path to make an initial loop that includes a good approach to the riverbank. Reaching nearly the end of this dike path, swing left to drop down to the parallel trail returning downstream towards your starting

FROM ABOVE The clear still waters of the river in midsummer; Small beach and shallow back channel.

point. Make a short trip on a side trail for a pretty view of the river. Passing a fine mess of blackberry bushes, carry on back in the direction of your starting point to complete this first loop.

2. Returning to the dike trail for only a few short metres, swing right to descend gently towards the river and some stands of fine, large cottonwoods. In a very short distance you will come to one of the two best approaches to the river. Here the bank is usually almost like sand, and a gravel bar creates a natural pool separated from the main river (though conditions vary from year to year and season to season). Erosion along the trail just past this point has necessitated a short but clearly indicated detour. Cross a pretty little footbridge, and, within a few minutes, come to a convergence of trails with a nicely positioned park bench. Ignore the broad, tempting-looking trail forking gradually right: it comes to a dead end at a battery of private property signs.

3. Having reconnected with the dike trail, swing gently right. Within a short distance you will come to a particularly interesting viewing platform on the left of the path. This one not only provides lots of fascinating information about waterfowl but also gives a leafy window onto a pretty marsh and pond and, almost inevitably, the ducky life it has tempted to visit.

4. Now comes the least natural part of the walk, but, for some at least, the most "educational." Passing on your left two more gentle ramps to parking areas, you will pass a park bench, a welcoming sign and – strange to say – a (malodorous!) view of the city's sewage treatment pools.

5. It is unlikely you will linger here. Instead, retrace your route to the junction just past the duck pond you just visited. Rather than descend to the river path on your left, keep atop the dike path to find another well-presented series of signs, these ones about animals like frogs, salamanders and

raccoons. Within a few metres after this spot, fork downwards to leave the dike trail.

6. As you swing right to go around a sports field on your left, note the potentially welcome presence of a drinking fountain. Ignore the trail leading into the trees on your right and carry on past the sports field. At this spot, approaching your starting point, swing right to cross a little bridge, and in no time at all you will see your waiting vehicle.

15. MT. TZOUHALEM CROSS TRAIL

*For a more challenging hike up the opposite end of the
Mt. Tzouhalem ridge, see Popular Day Hikes 4: Vancouver
Island. The hike described here is by far the most popular
walking route through a maze of mountain-biking trails.
The destination is a ridgetop with beautifully gardenlike
clusters of arbutus amidst interesting rock formations,
all with spectacular views of the Cowichan Valley.*

LOCATION

From Highway 1 in central
Duncan, turn east at the Co-op
Gas Station onto Trunk Road.
Drive for about 1.2 km until it
turns into Tzouhalem Road. Continue straight ahead for about
1 km. When you come to a roundabout, go straight through to
the second exit, onto Maple Bay
Road. Drive for 3 km and turn
right onto Kingsview Road. After
about 200 m, come to another
roundabout. Keep on Kingsview
Road for another 1 km until you
come to Chippewa Road. Turn
right and continue for 1 km, and
then turn left onto Kaspa Road
and drive about 450 m until
you see the large, signposted
parking area.

DISTANCE

6.3 km

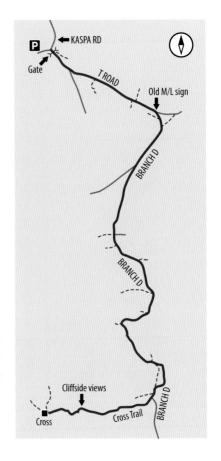

ELEVATION GAIN
95 m

DIFFICULTY
Moderate. Most of the trail is on an old roadbed. The last section is narrow, irregular and a bit rooty but without any significant challenges. The cliffs at the top could be dangerous for foolhardy visitors.

SEASON
All season, though be aware that in winter, if you find it chilly, but clear, at the bottom of the mountain there could be some snow at the top. Just look up! April is great for spring flowers, but mostly at the ecological reserve partway up, along a more convoluted route than that described here.

OF SPECIAL INTEREST FOR CHILDREN
Probably more interesting for kids than the vertiginous views (though, of course, children enjoy gasping and being restrained from throwing things off cliffs) is the cluttered community of rock sculptures partway up the route. Think: inuksuk. The implicit invitation to contribute to the growing crowd is clear! Stronger, older children could ride their (mountain) bikes most – but not all – of the route.

Note that if you come on a weekend or holiday, you can often just follow the other families taking this popular route.

---

1. Facing uphill, walk to the left end of the parking lot, passing by a yellow gate. Ignore a branch off to your right going up to a water tower. Carry on up a broad, gravel road, ignoring a downhill track on your left. After a short distance fork left to continue uphill.

2. At the next fork, see a sign saying "Old M/L" (i.e., old main line), and a smaller road to the right. Go right onto a smaller

CLOCKWISE FROM ABOVE LEFT The cliffs drop precipitously from a high spot overlooking the farms and fields of the Cowichan Valley; river estuaries at the end of Cowichan Bay; the rock city partway along the most popular route to the summit.

track with a sign, "Branch D," high on a tree. This track traverses gradually uphill through a typical second-growth Douglas fir forest – phalanxes of tall, thin, crowded trees above a bed of salal.

3. A treat, however, awaits. Ignoring tracks first to the right and then the left, keeping straight ahead on Branch D, after a time, you come upon a charming chaos of improvised rock towers, cairns and some wonderfully bizarre rock structures. Thereafter, while your route tends generally smoothly uphill, you come upon one steep, rocky section of roadbed before descending.

4. At a low point, fork right onto a narrow, rooty trail through ferns, and again right where you see the trail broadening out and heading slightly uphill. There is light ahead, and it comes from the clearing running along the broken, angular edge of the ramp-like mountain.

5. Although you may be tempted to feel you have reached your airy, view-rich destination, even better sights await you. Turn right and take the wandering, clear trail along the top of the cliffs of conglomerate rock. Exclaim to your heart's content over the attractive arrangements of broken stone and arbutus. Press on to the point where the cliff trail brings you out to a viewpoint that allows you to look back along the curve of the mountain edge – as well, of course, as down on the full sweep of the Cowichan Valley. Some will find the large Christian cross there to be intrusive, others inspirational – in either case, it's one of those can't-miss-it insertions into the landscape.

6. It is possible to follow a loop route down through the conservation area (you see a sign for the border), but, largely because of the complexities of this route, the great majority of visitors return the way they came and take an opportunity to add their own creative touches to the rock village.

16. BALD MOUNTAIN

A post-logging-devastation version of what used to be one of the most beloved ascents on Vancouver Island. Fortunately, enough time has passed since the clear-cutting, and the views are attractive enough that the current trails make for a great family outing.

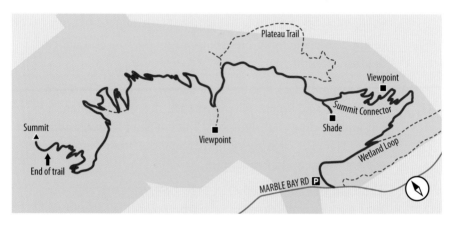

LOCATION
From Duncan, take Cowichan Valley Highway (18 West). Arriving at Lake Cowichan, take North Shore Road. Turn left onto Meades Creek Road and drive for 1.5 km, and then turn right onto Marble Bay Road and proceed for 2.3 km. Turn into a large gravel parking area on your right. Notice the sign and map.

DISTANCE
8-km return

ELEVATION GAIN
340 m

DIFFICULTY
The trail builders rate the trail as "moderately difficult," largely, no doubt, because of the considerable gain in altitude. The fact

Hemlocks frame the view east on Cowichan Lake.

that families with fairly small children regularly galumph along the trail, though, says a lot. A sign at one point warns of dangerous cliffs, but the cliffs are well beyond a bend in the trail.

SEASON

All season. Because the logging company has swept clean most trees off this once-iconic mountain, the climb can be baking hot in summer.

OF SPECIAL INTEREST FOR CHILDREN

The climb is significant enough, and the views dramatic enough, that (motivated) children may well like the sense of accomplishment that comes with the climb (though the trail doesn't quite go to the high spot).

1. Passing the signs and map, begin on Woodland Trail, rising gently through the broom-lined, broad path traversing the south slope of the mountain.

2. If you have very little walkers on your outing, you can continue on this trail to make a short loop back to your starting point (along Wetland Loop). For the route to the top, turn up well-flagged Summit Connector.

3. This trail gains you considerable altitude fairly quickly, switchbacking through young Douglas firs, hemlocks and, of course, stumps. Very soon, you have a good view over the east end of Cowichan Lake. After levelling off, the trail heads towards the now-visible high point, before coming to a junction with Plateau Trail. (This trail offers you a loop around a knoll and reconnects with Summit Connector Trail farther along.) If you're sweltering under relentless sun, take heart: there is a short, signposted trail to some much-needed shade under a few larger firs.

4. The most deservedly popular route, straight ahead, gains only slight altitude until, after passing the northern end of Plateau Trail you come to the junction with the signposted Upper Summit Trail, really just the extension of the main trail. You may wish to postpone turning onto Upper Summit Trail until you've wandered a little past the junction to a kind of official viewpoint and bench – and some shade. Be careful not to wander onto old logging roads, watching for signposts directing you to Summit Trail (as it is called on these posts).

5. After crossing an old logging road, you find the terrain becomes a little looser and steeper at a few points on the next section as you rise, via switchbacks, along the northeast side of the ridge. Take time to appreciate the occasional views over this arm of Cowichan Lake, since you lose this perspective well before the "summit" (so-called because it's a summit of the close end of the ridge rather than the whole mountain).

6. The trail tends increasingly west as you begin switchbacking up the steepest slope of the mountain – though you must decide whether to follow the official switchbacks rising gradually or use the much more popular and well-trodden

One of the most attractive parts of the trail, in part because it escaped the logging zone.

FROM LEFT The view south from near the summit; the view towards Youbou from near the summit.

shortcuts cutting more steeply up the slope. For the sake of both view and your oxygen levels, you probably want to pause when the trail levels out. The (rickety) bench may prove to be very welcome. The views along the lake, through some droopy but attractive hemlocks, are especially lovely. Brace yourself for the push to the (sort of) summit!

7. Skirting some rocky buttresses, and entering some comparatively large trees, the trail traverses horizontally around the mountain towards the south arm of the lake. You – and small, stumbling children – should be a little careful along this section, since the rocky slope is quite steep (though not dangerous). The final push to the high point brings you through lodgepole pines and even some junipers, normally native only to the most sunbaked and rocky land. A little dishearteningly, a signpost leans exhaustedly, announcing the end of the maintained trail, just a little before the high point. The good news is that you can easily tromp through the rough grass and sparse trees to an approximation of a high point with views in nearly all directions.

8. Return to your vehicle the way you came – though, if you have excess energy, you can take Plateau Trail loop on your way down.

17. HONEYMOON BAY ECOLOGICAL RESERVE

A tiny gem, this moss-shrouded forest, beautiful in itself, is particularly remarkable for its springtime display of pink fawn lilies and other wild flowers.

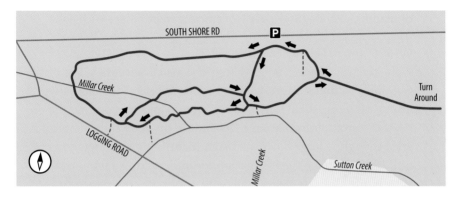

LOCATION

From central Cowichan Lake village, drive about 13 km along South Shore Road. Almost exactly 1 km before your destination you will see the entrance to Gordon Bay Provincial Park on your right. Look for a small gravel parking area and a broad trailhead marked with a large, irregular boulder.

DISTANCE

2.1 km partial loop, with shorter variations possible.

ELEVATION GAIN

Negligible

DIFFICULTY

Almost entirely easy, level paths, though a little narrow at some spots. Getting onto the bouldery bank of Millar Creek might require a little care.

SEASON

Almost any season is walkable, though the star attraction of this little reserve, the display of pink fawn lilies, is usually at its best in early spring. Amongst the other wildflowers that thrive here – trilliums, violets and, a little later, bleeding hearts – are particularly good at spreading the flowery joy. Given the number of maples, October and early November can be ablaze with gold.

OF SPECIAL INTEREST FOR CHILDREN

Note that picnicking and cycling, the usual surefire ways of tweaking a child's interest, are not allowed here. (In fact, any group of more than ten requires special permission via the posted contact information.) Depending on your child's interests, though, a large illustrated sign identifying the huge array of flowers could be the instigation for undertaking a floral treasure hunt. The safe, level trails and confined area mean, too, that even young children can safely run ahead and wait for their more sedate parents.

1. From the trailhead turn right in the clearing to enjoy the large illustrated sign and note the simple bench, potentially welcome later in the visit. For a short visit you can confine your walk to the Alec Walker Memorial Loop Trail, a little under 1 km long. Having sampled the beauties of this remarkable forest bordered by a pretty creek, however, you almost certainly will want to explore further, especially since doing so will allow you to walk along the loveliest part of the trail twice, but in opposite directions. For either the shorter or the longer version, though, begin by turning left past the big sign and walking towards Sutton Creek through a rich array of sword ferns. After a short distance, notice the smaller trail branching to the right – you will be using this trail on the full walk. For now, though, go straight ahead to the bank of Sutton Creek, viewed through a lattice of tree boughs.

2. It is worth dropping down into the creek bed to enjoy the view both downstream and upstream along and across the creek. Return to the path and follow its curves and bends upstream along the edge of the largely hemlock and maple forest. At some other points it is possible to go down to the streambed, though the reserve wardens sometimes post signs closing those routes, especially if winter floods have made them difficult or even dangerous. As you approach the west end of the reserve, notice a small trail leading to the right, but for now carry on straight ahead (trying to avoid the sight of logging-road maintenance equipment which may be visible ahead through the trees).

3. The Alec Walker Trail swings away from the creek, towards the road, and then curves back towards your starting point and roughly parallel to the road. Along this section notice the particularly large rotten stumps, the last traces of former giants. At the same time, make a point of walking slowly and looking straight up to the canopy: the trees here are not huge in diameter but they do make for an inspiring sense of height.

4. Back at the starting point, convinced now that you want to enjoy more of this spot, turn right to go the short distance to the small trail branching right and running through the centre of the forest. As you walk along this central trail you will pass two of the largest trees in the reserve, both firs, but also some wonderfully contorted maples. Fans of fantasy fiction will have a hard time restraining their imagination.

5. Concluding your exploration of this narrow central path and coming back to the shoreline section of the Alec Walker Trail, turn left to enjoy this prettiest trail again. You almost certainly will notice features from this different angle that you missed on the way out. This time, when you reach the point where the Alec Walker Loop swings away from Sutton

FROM LEFT Hemlock and moss-covered stumps create an emerald green world; Pink fawn lilies and yellow violets bloom in April.

Creek, instead of going back to the entrance, turn right to enjoy an entirely new section of forest.

6. When you come to a T-junction, you will have another decision to make. The trail on your right ends within a few minutes' walk. You will notice, however, by the fact that it is well trodden, that many visitors are happy to extend their enjoyment even though it means going out and back along this trail and, for a short section, leaving the reserve. Remarkable for its combination of hemlock and maple, this dead-end trail is even more remarkable for an unusual feature at your turnaround spot (a spot marked by a "no entry" sign). Before turning back, take time to appreciate the double-trunked hemlock growing out of the huge, rotten "nurse" stump.

7. Once back at the T-junction, turn right to walk the short distance back to the main trailhead and your car.

18. STONEY HILL

A winding trail over arbutus bluffs in Stoney Hill
Regional Park to a series of high-elevation views
over Samsun Narrows and Salt Spring Island.

LOCATION

From the highway in downtown
Duncan, at a set of traffic lights,
turn east onto Trunk Road.
After just over 1 km, continue
along Tzouhalem Road for an
additional 1 km. When you
come to a roundabout, take the
second exit for Maple Bay Road
and drive 5.5 km. Turn right
onto Genoa Bay Road and go
just over 5 km until you see a

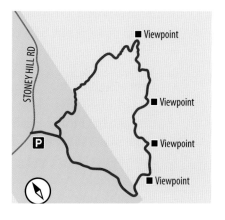

sign for Stoney Hill on your left. Climb the newly paved road
for about 1 km and come to a clearly marked parking area on
the right.

DISTANCE

3.2-km loop

ELEVATION GAIN

Approximately 90 m, cumulative (217-m high point)

DIFFICULTY

A generally well-developed and graded trail. One end of the loop
is signed as "moderate" and the other as "easy." The moderate
end is steeper and more irregular but otherwise not challenging.

SEASON

All season, but good weather makes for by far the best views.
Some squelchy spots are bypassed by small, improvised trails.

OF SPECIAL INTEREST FOR CHILDREN

While nothing stands out as of special interest, most kids would vastly prefer this trail to simply a walk in the woods – the many viewpoints have enough of a clifflike gasp factor that most children should feel a thrill. Children who struggle to see the point in slogging uphill, too, will get maximum sense of elevation with minimum effort: the trail starts at a high point. Your kids' pooch is welcome here – but only on leash. Most important, perhaps, are several perfect picnic spots.

1. Pass a sign saying "Temporary Entrance" (with no indication of when this might change) and begin a gradual ascent through firs on a broad dirt track. Within a few minutes, you come to a T junction and signposts indicating blue (moderately difficult) left and green (easy) right. Begin the loop by turning right. A short way along, ignore a mossy roadbed to the right and follow the signposts left past a big old maple and lots of alders.

2. As you ascend gradually, pass some deep beds of moss before coming to a stack of small logs directly in front of a wet area, put there to direct you to a narrow bypass trail on the right, past a picturesque mossy bluff – the first of many ragged chunks of sandstone on and near the top of the aptly called Stoney Hill. Soon after, be aware of the trees on your right becoming increasingly sparse and allowing tempting viewpoints just off the trail. For whatever reason, however, a signpost insists that you not leave the trail to a viewpoint but, instead, that you "Stay on Trail" by swinging left and keeping inside a line of boulders.

3. Rewarding views await. After sauntering along a particularly lovely bit of open woods, a small pond and past another Stay on Trail sign, you come to some *Ooh* and *Ahh* views over Samsun Narrows and towards Salt Spring Island's Mt. Maxwell. Even better, this is not the only view you're going to get: though the trail starts to drop and lead away from the

CLOCKWISE FROM LEFT The well-marked trail on the northeast side of the hill; the view over Samsun Narrows; Salt Spring Island and Mt. Maxwell.

cliffs, it will bring you back to other viewpoints and, after winding through an amazing cluster of arbutus, to one particularly large bluff with sweeping views.

4. From here the trail snakes through salal and firs towards and down an increasingly steep bank. Levelling out, it continues to amble through lovely open trees until the narrow trail becomes a broader track. A signpost points you left around a grove of (invasive but pretty) holly and bit of bog. In case you thought it was all downhill from here, you're wrong. A slight climb over a crest, down and across a little bridge, around a potentially wet spot, and you're back to the beginning of the loop.

19. BRIGHT ANGEL PARK

An impressive suspension bridge over a tranquil,
deep, easily accessible river and a network
of paths through a forest of large fir.

LOCATION

About 9 km south of Duncan on Highway 1, turn onto Bench Road. Drive about 1.7 km and take a sharp right onto Koksilah Road. After just over 1 km, turn right onto Tigwell Road and drive just over 0.5 km. Follow the signpost for Bright Angel Regional Park and park at the first parking lot beside a playing field.

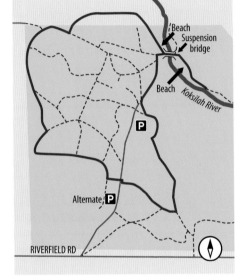

DISTANCE

1.7-km route through a network (many options)

ELEVATION GAIN

50 m

DIFFICULTY

Mostly easy, broad, smooth paths, except for one rooty, wet section on the river.

SEASON

All season, though summer is obviously best to take advantage of the potential for water play; even in a dry summer, the river pools remain reasonably deep.

The graceful suspension bridge from the viewpoint of a favourite swimming spot.

OF SPECIAL INTEREST FOR CHILDREN

The impressive suspension bridge is good fun. Few are the children who won't take a keen interest in the easy access to the river. While most of the trails are suitable for chunky-tire cycling, bicycles are not allowed. Picnic facilities and toilets make the park particularly suitable for small children.

1. Pass the large posted map of the park and take the first gravel track to the right, sloping gradually downhill (signposted with an icon for swimming). The trail sweeps around to run along the forested bank of the river with a park bench overlooking the woodsy scene.

2. Within no distance, come to the wood-planked suspension bridge high over the deep pools of the river. Kids will want to dawdle over the bridge, of course, but, once you are across, turn right to explore a dirt trail running several hundred metres upstream.

3. A sometimes uneven trail runs parallel to the shore, at some points with a split-cedar fence where the bank is eroded. Some beautiful large cedars and firs shade the enticing little beach during the morning: plan your visit with that in mind. The trail peters out when it comes to a gravel bar and cliff. Return to the bridge. (You may wish to explore a little

Another good swimming beach downstream from the suspension bridge.

downstream from the bridge, but the trail doesn't go very far in this direction.)

4. Back across the bridge, ignore the broad track up the hill and instead turn right to walk downstream. In a short distance, come to a pleasant gravel beach with another opportunity to get any feet wet that are still dry. Keep right, turning uphill along a broad trail, to climb around the north end of the park, pausing to admire some particularly large cottonwoods. This well-used section of the trail, not quite within park boundaries, can get quite muddy in winter.

5. Ignore a broad trail on your right (leading downhill to the beginning of a road), then three smaller trails in succession on your left. Keep ahead to swing behind the playing field along a well-groomed section of the trail (part of the so-called fitness loop).

6. Cross the asphalt road to take the signposted next section of the fitness loop. This crushed-gravel trail winds towards the riverbank then curves downstream but well back from the river. En route, keep left when you come to a fork with a broad downward track on your right. After passing some character trees and a large (seasonal) pond on your left, find yourself soon back at the parking lot and your vehicle.

20. COBBLE HILL

A well-used route through Cobble Hill Mountain Regional Recreation Area, amongst a network of trails starting in a rainforest ecosystem and ending at a high point of arbutus, rocky bluffs and views over the Gulf Islands.

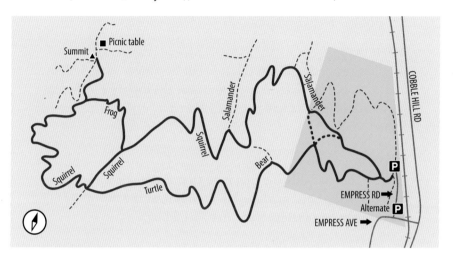

LOCATION

Cobble Hill Road is a loop road off Highway 1 between Duncan and Mill Bay. If you are driving south on Highway 1, the road is prominently signposted at a set of traffic lights beside a shopping plaza (Valley View Centre) and Cowichan Bay Road. From this intersection, drive 2.5 km along Cobble Hill Road.

If you are driving north on Highway 1, look for a Petro-Canada station on your left as you leave Mill Bay and then turn left at the traffic lights onto Cobble Hill Road. Drive 4.4 km.

Driving from either direction, you see a park and parking lot right next to Cobble Hill Road. Turn onto Empress Avenue, nearly opposite Olde School Coffee. Drive a short distance up Empress Avenue and turn into the signposted park along Empress Road.

Park in the parking lot for Quarry Park, the farthest parking lot from Empress Avenue.

DISTANCE
5.4-km loop

ELEVATION GAIN
215 m

DIFFICULTY
Families regularly hike to the top, but be aware: some huffing and puffing is involved. A few spots near the top are a little slippery with loose dirt and pebbles, as well as dry arbutus leaves (mostly in July).

SEASON
All year, but as with any hill, note that if there is a sprinkling of snow at the bottom of the hill in winter, at the top of the hill there might be a little more than a sprinkling.

OF SPECIAL INTEREST FOR CHILDREN
An unusual feature of these trails is that they have been graded with cute little signs for various animals (primarily intended as guides for mountain bikers). Finding the next squirrel on the way up – and, on the way down, frogs, tortoises and bunnies – can be huge fun. (Be aware: Not all these signs are always in place.) Other than that, there is a picnic table at a great viewpoint – and we all know what is best done at picnic tables! Although this trail is indicated as an easy mountain-biking trail, only older children with tough little legs and downhill skills will find it bike-able.

1. The first part of your route is in Quarry Nature Park. Head gradually uphill on a gravel service road until, after a very short distance, you see your friend, the squirrel, pointing your way to the right. This broad, well-tramped trail, though a little rooty in places, will take you through sword ferns and large cedars. When you come to a cross trail and a post

CLOCKWISE FROM ABOVE The view towards the Gulf Islands from the picnic table at the summit; looking south from the summit; an impressive old Douglas fir beside the first part of the trail.

with another squirrel image, you may (justifiably) be a little puzzled since it is not at all clear whether the sign indicates that you are to turn right or go straight ahead. To which trail does the sign apply? As it turns out, such signs, without arrows, mean go straight ahead. In a few steps, notice a sign indicating you have crossed into a regional district area, confirming you have made the right decision!

2. In a few minutes, come to another junction, but this time the trusty wee squirrel has arrows indicating that, indeed, you go straight ahead. Yet another intersection a short distance on comes complete with choice of animals: ignore the poor salamander to your right and go left to follow Mr. Squirrel through two dramatic switchbacks. Don't be so eager to find the next sign, however, that you go right past a particularly magnificent Douglas fir on the left of the path.

3. Eager as you may be to get to the top of the mountain, don't turn onto the frog path at your next junction, even though the squirrel path seems to be not only levelling out but even taking you slightly downhill. Persevere past a park bench, and soon find your trusty squirrel, at a cross path heading almost directly uphill to your right. (This time, as it happens, the sign without benefit of directional arrows means that you turn onto a new trail.)

4. Winding through many turns up the slope, you soon find yourself increasingly into the arbutus-zone characteristic of the top part of the hill. Forge on ahead past an unsignposted trail marked with red paint splotches on trees. Passing more squirrel signs, note a frog sign as you pass it, since you do return to this point on your downhill route.

5. Watch your footing over some potentially slippery bits of the last part of the trail. Soon you pop out of the trees into an open area dotted with small trees and some exotic little manzanita bushes. Explore this area of glades a little, heading left to get the best views south towards Shawnigan Lake.

Many trails wander temptingly off in various directions from here, but be warned: signposts are few here, and most of these trails lead to long, confusing loops that do, eventually, lead back to your starting point – but only eventually. For the picnic table and views of Salt Spring Island, wander your way to the north end of the summit area.

6. Ready to head home? Return the way you came until you come to the frog trail. Several sharp little switchbacks on the frog trail take you quickly down, out of the arbutus zone to join the squirrel trail you used on the way up. Turn right to repeat the next short section of traversing trail past the bench.

7. When you come to the cross trail this time, turn left to follow the turtle route, twisting and turning through several bends and increasingly large trees. Children who feel they have had enough of turtles may be surprised that a different kind of sign suddenly announces that – temporarily at least – the turtle trail has become the bear trail. The two animals are clearly in competition: farther along, you pass another turtle sign and, yes, another bear sign, this time as you pass a large water tank.

8. Turn down a broad dirt road to an intersection where you pass a venerable chunk of logging equipment and, at an intersection, a sign for the rabbit trail. Possibly without your noticing, you have re-entered Quarry Nature Park. It is only a short rabbit-hop the rest of the way to the parking lot.

21. KOKSILAH TRAILS

Clear trails and deep, emerald-green pools beneath sculpted rock formations – and connections to long-distance trails (including Kinsol Trestle). Like many provincial parks, Koksilah has scant evidence of maintenance or development.

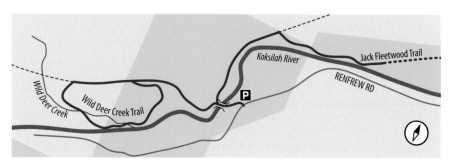

LOCATION
From Highway 1 in Mill Bay, turn at the traffic lights away from the water onto Shawnigan Lake/Mill Bay Road. When you get to the T junction by Shawnigan Lake, turn right at the end of the lake, then left onto Renfrew Road. Follow Renfrew Road past Shawnigan Lake, which continues after the road becomes gravel. Koksilah Provincial Park is signposted on a carved wooden sign, but don't expect any park amenities other than a well-used but slightly chaotic dirt parking area.

DISTANCE
2.3-km return (plus 1.6-km return optional add-on)

ELEVATION GAIN
30 m

DIFFICULTY
No steep grades or exposed positions, but trails can be rough and eroded. BC Parks describes these as "rustic"!

SEASON

Any season, but summer is especially good, since, even with decreasing river flow at the end of a hot summer, the pools remain deep and luscious. In winter, crossing Wild Deer Creek can be a little...wet.

OF SPECIAL INTEREST FOR CHILDREN

Deep and luscious pools? What child can resist? Easy beach access to smaller pools and lots of opportunities for clambering over boulders make this a great destination for family water play. Be aware that there are no facilities.

1. Prepare yourself for the most bizarre entrance to a provincial park you are likely to encounter. The park is across the river from the parking spot, and you must make your way to a large, gated logging-road bridge and crawl through the gaps in the gate before crossing the bridge to the park.

2. From the bridge, the views of the river's convolutions and deep bowls are little short of amazing. Once across the bridge, stop to read the map of the park and volunteer-made trails leading all the way downstream to the Kinsol Trestle, and beyond. Walk the few steps up to an old gravel roadbed and turn left past the sign for Wild Deer Creek Trail. Start with a bit of a tromp, and a not particularly uplifting one, through small second-growth Douglas firs until you see a broad gravel trail below the road on the left. The proper (signposted) trailhead for your trail is farther along the road ahead. However, impatient folk have beaten a well-worn shortcut down the bank to the trail.

3. Whichever way you get onto Wild Deer Creek Trail, turn left to begin a long descending trail curving to your right and bringing you to your first riverside vantage point. While this spot is pleasant enough, other spots a little farther upstream are probably more attractive and do have deeper pools.

CLOCKWISE FROM ABOVE LEFT The water remains crystal clear, except during winter storms; looking downstream from the bridge; The deepest pools are upstream from the access bridge; many deep pools remain, even at the end of a hot summer.

4. Regain the loop part of the trail, now running parallel to the Koksilah River and bringing you, past some large maples, to some other riverside spots good for picnicking, getting wet and so on. Once you've enjoyed what the river or your lunch pack has to offer, turn away from the trail to continue your loop walk. Soon you understand why the trail is named as it is. As two park signs will tell you, not only might you have to cross the creek bed but the creek bed is part of Wild Deer Creek.

5. The trail will deliver you back onto the old logging road, a couple of hundred metres away from the start of the loop. Make the easy stroll back to the bridge and your starting point.

Optional Add-On: Jack Fleetwood Trail

If you have the energy and curiosity to explore, on your return from Wild Deer Creek, carry on past the bridge along the gravel road for a few hundred metres. The road rises high above the river and is well back from it. When you come to Jack Fleetwood Trail, however, a beautifully built wooden raised staircase makes for an interesting and attractive descent to the river flats. Here, you can wander along a lovely trail surrounded by sword ferns and through firs and maples. This first section of trail is closest to the river, allowing you to get a good view of the largely bouldery, splashy water. Shortly after crossing a little bridge, the trail reaches perhaps the closest vantage point onto the river before heading away. You may wish to use this as your turn around spot since, from here, the trail, though reasonably pretty, is far away from the river. On the other hand, you may have planned for a bit of an adventure and arranged for a pickup at the Kinsol Trestle, 5 km distant. (See the Kinsol Trestle description next for the combination of trails at the other end.)

22. KINSOL TRESTLE & JACK FLEETWOOD (EAST) TRAIL

An astoundingly high and long wooden trestle above a forested gorge, leading to winding trails down to and along the Koksilah River. The reconstructed historic trestle, named for the King Solomon mining company, is the largest wooden trestle in the Commonwealth, and one of the longest in the world.

LOCATION

From Mill Bay on Highway 1, turn onto Shawnigan Lake/Mill Bay Road and drive about 6 km to the head of Shawnigan Lake and the intersection with Renfrew Road. After travelling 6.5 km along Renfrew Road, turn right onto Glen Eagles Road and drive 1.5 km to the signposted parking lot for the trestle trail.

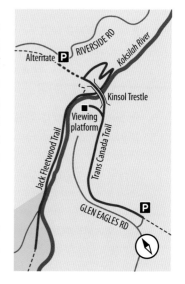

DISTANCE

3-km return from river; approximately 5-km return from Jack Fleetwood Trail intersection

ELEVATION GAIN

45 m

DIFFICULTY

Extremely easy walk to the trail along the Trans Canada Trail section. The trail down to the river and under the trestle is smooth and well-graded, but, of course, involves a bit of heavy breathing. Jack Fleetwood (east) Trail along the Koksilah River becomes narrow, rocky and irregular at points. The official warning is that the trail is "technical" and requires "proper footwear," but there is no need to be intimidated by the warning.

The Koksilah River near the beginning of Jack Fleetwood Trail.

SEASON
All season

OF SPECIAL INTEREST FOR CHILDREN
As long as nervousness of heights doesn't outweigh the giddy pleasure of being so very high, most kids should be thrilled. Riding bikes along the Trans Canada Trail over the bridge and in either direction is an option, but scotch any ideas of taking bikes down the switchbacks and/or along Jack Fleetwood Trail.

1. Join the merry throngs (and, during pleasant weather, "throngs" is not much of an exaggeration) making their way along the level, wide former railroad bed, now the Trans Canada Trail.

2. When you come to the trestle, take the short trail you see leading down to the left to the jutting viewpoint – but be aware you can't get to the bottom of the trestle from this trail. Return to the main trail at the top and, of course, go to the very middle of the trestle to indulge in gasps of amazement and, if that's your style, a little dark humour.

3. Crossing the trestle, take the trail to the right. This will bring you, via three large, carefully graded switchbacks, to the bottom of the trestle and the most impressive viewpoints on the structure, size, sweep, design and so on. For some, this will be the destination and the turning point.

4. For others, who would like to explore a little farther, take the trail upstream, walking cheerfully past the sign warning against the "technical" difficulties that await. Ignore the trail on your right, which does not show on the official map of the area (leading, quite steeply, to the Trans Canada Trail). First come to a lovely little riverside spot with enough deep, clear water to get everyone and their dog thoroughly wet.

5. If you're a little confused by the name of the trail because you have been to Koksilah Provincial Park, you will be satisfied to know that, as, indeed, you remember, there is a trail there, also called Jack Fleetwood Trail, in that case leading to the Can Am Trail – which runs parallel to (but not close to) the Koksilah River. All you need to remember, for your purposes, is to enjoy the walk along this little winding trail through some lovely forest, over two small wooden bridges, until you reach a T junction with the Can Am Trail. Although it is possible to turn right and make your way ultimately to the Trans Canada Trail, and from there back to the trestle, probably the best and pleasantest way back is simply returning along the riverside Jack Fleetwood Trail.

CLOCKWISE FROM ABOVE The trestle from the viewing spot closest to the parking lot; the view into the canyon from the middle of the trestle; one of the small bridges along this end of the Jack Fleetwood Trail.

23. OLD BALDY

Not to be confused with Bald Mountain by Cowichan Lake, this rounded series of exposed bluffs above Shawnigan Lake has splendid views in nearly all directions.

LOCATION

From the centre of Mill Bay on Highway 1, turn onto Shawnigan Lake/Mill Bay Road and drive for 3.5 km. Take a left turn onto Sylvester Road and drive for 1.3 km. Turn right onto Baldy Mountain Road and, after 850 m, turn onto Hawking Road and drive 2.2 km, until you see a gravel road on your left with a yellow gate (about 100 m after a house numbered 1754).

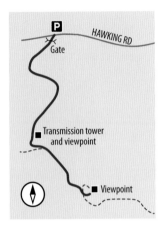

DISTANCE

2.2 km

ELEVATION GAIN

220 m (458-m summit elevation)

DIFFICULTY

The gravel approach road to the first excellent viewpoint is easy. The route to the summit does require a little scrambling (and a little use of hands) over rocky bluffs, but on a clearly marked trail and with no precipitous drops. Since there are some fairly steep cliffs off the trail, children's enthusiasm for romping off trail should be constrained.

SEASON

All season, but choose a clear day for the best view. Remember that in winter there may be a little snow at the top even if there is none at the base.

CLOCKWISE FROM TOP Looking north along Shawnigan Lake; Salt Spring Island and the Saanich Peninsula from the summit; berry-covered arbutus frame a late-summer view of the south end of the lake.

OF SPECIAL INTEREST FOR CHILDREN

The second half of the trail, with its airy feeling, rocky bits of scrambling and accessible summit, should create a sense of real adventure for most children. This is not a sedate stroll with The Parents. The bluffs also make an ideal picnic spot.

1. Pass by the yellow gate and immediately begin a gradual ascent up a gravel service road. The road makes three long switchbacks through small, scrubby growth until you see, looming ahead, a very functional-looking cluster of aerials, towers and a metal hut.

2. Stop at this spot to wander a little. If you can ignore the unlovely bits of communication technology, you can get some surprisingly lovely views over the north end of Shawnigan Lake and the low mountains beyond.

3. Though the trail on from here is well-worn, the trailhead can be a little hard to spot. Turn back to a faded-green utility pole and notice the rocky track slightly obscured by some low scrub. This first part of the trail takes you within a few easy minutes to an open area of smooth, rounded rock surrounded by arbutus. The view to the south end of the lake and beyond is the stuff of calendar photos!

4. Ignore a path to your right. This steep path is an alternate way up the mountain to reach this point. Although coming this way does allow you to avoid walking up the service road, it is too difficult to be considered a family walk, unless your last name is Hillary. Your own adventure lies ahead. Though safe enough, the trail climbs over several steep sections of exposed rock. Spot a few manzanita bushes, looking for all the world like miniature arbutus.

5. Just before the summit the trail levels out onto another open, airy view area, giving you probably the best views of the south end of the lake. Turning towards the very rounded summit, you see a rough bit of service road. While this leads up to the summit by going left, the trail leading straight across it takes you quickly to your goal.

6. While the summit area has been chewed up to provide a level area of broken rock, if you wander its perimeter you can treat yourself to some great views in all directions – even over Salt Spring Island and the Saanich Peninsula.

7. After exchanging congratulations and eating your well-deserved cookies, return the way you came.

24. SPECTACLE LAKE

*A loop in Spectacle Lake Provincial Park around a small
lake with a diverse shoreline, including rocky bluffs,
marsh and a small swimming beach.*

LOCATION
Almost 11 km north of Goldstream Provincial
Park on Highway 1 (the Malahat), you see the
well-signposted turn for Spectacle Lake Provincial Park onto Whittaker Road. About 300 m
along, turn left to stay on Whittaker Road, again
signposted for the park. After about 800 m, fork
right to follow the signs a short distance to the
parking lot.

DISTANCE
2.4 km

ELEVATION GAIN
Negligible

DIFFICULTY
Easy, but with a few stumbly bits and pieces of roots and rocks
on the west side (the return part of the loop suggested here).

SEASON
All season, though obviously beach season has appeal.

OF SPECIAL INTEREST FOR CHILDREN
Be a little wary of the sign indicating the trail is suitable for
biking. It isn't – at least not all the way around (though the east
side is easy and broad). The small swimming beach is an obvious
magnet. And the picnic tables are there for a reason.

1. You'll probably want to look at the pretty little beach (and
    who cares that it is artificial?) where the trail from the

The view from the rocky bluffs on the east side of the lake

parking lot first reaches the lake. For obvious practical reasons you may want to postpone any watery pleasures you or the young 'uns have in mind and, noting the potential usefulness of the waste bin and outhouse, head off to the right of the beach. Here you pick up a broad, level and smooth roadbed running parallel to the east shore of the lake.

2. When, after a short distance, you see a small trail leading towards the lake, take it. Otherwise, you'll be missing out on one of the prettiest sections of the walk. Experiencing the rounded, rocky bluffs with patches of moss and the view up and down the lake, you may find the words "picture perfect" floating across your mind.

3. Swinging away from the lake to the main trail, continue to the end of the lake. The trail changes character as it passes behind the marsh, through some alders and over an attractively curving bridge. Pass through some large cedars and over a second bridge.

The small beach near the parking lot is a popular swimming spot in summer

4. Now you are on the shady southwest side of the long, narrow lake. The comparatively narrow and uneven trail along this side of the lake will take you over a boardwalk and up through small firs to rocky bluffs. Although the lake is partly screened by trees along this section, small side trails lead to viewpoints. A park bench beside two magisterial firs encourages you to pause and solve some the world's more pressing problems.

5. Continue on the clear, well-marked trail as it drops to low ground and brings you back to your starting point. Time to break out the bathing suits and/or peanut butter and banana sandwiches.

25. NIAGARA FALLS & TRESTLE WALK

*Two easily accessible Wow-factor treats in
Goldstream Provincial Park, linked by a dramatically
switchbacking trail through large trees.*

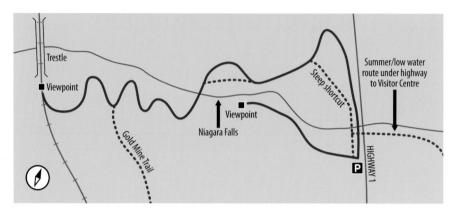

LOCATION

Goldstream Park is impossible to miss given that Highway 1 goes right through the middle of it. Driving north from Victoria, turn right off the highway and go to the parking lot closest to the Visitor Centre. This approach, however, is suitable only during the drier months. When the streams are running high (and the waterfall is most spectacular), safe and/or comfortable access to these trails is possible only if you are driving south. The small, signposted parking lot is on the right as the highway completes its descent from the Malahat.

DISTANCE
1.5-km return

ELEVATION GAIN
90 m

DIFFICULTY

This is probably not the best walk for small children with unco-ordinated limbs or for anyone nervous about heights. The trail to the falls is a little narrow, even slippery at times, and the climb to the trestle, though not long, is a bit of a grunt. As for the sky-high trestle itself – well, it is a sky-high trestle. A firm grip and/or obedient children are what you want.

SEASON

Summer for ease of visiting and general prettiness, autumn for combining walking with watching the chum salmon spawn, winter and spring for the most spectacular waterfall derring-do.

OF SPECIAL INTEREST FOR CHILDREN

Any child who is capable of being awed by height will be thrilled by the double heights, first of the falls, second of the trestle.

Step One: During Summer and Early Fall and/or When the Water Is Low

1. From the main parking lot, walk beyond the picnic area along the main trail. When you come to a fork, turn left towards the highway where a huge culvert/tunnel goes under the highway. Make your way through this tunnel on the left side of any flowing water, only easily passable if the water level is low. When you arrive at the stream at the other side, follow the uneven trail along the stream towards the waterfall until you meet the main trail from the parking lot up the stairs to your left.

Step One: Late Fall through Early Spring and/or When the Water Is High

1. Having approached from the Malahat and parked in the small signposted lot, walk towards the stream and descend the sequence of sturdy steps towards the creek.

Onward: All Season

2. First visit the falls from this side of the creek, appreciating the fact that not only is this one of the highest easily accessible falls on Vancouver Island but it also is one of the

FROM LEFT The entrance to the goldmine shaft; Niagara Falls is almost as high as the gigantic falls of the same name.

few where you can see the falls from a secure spot below the falls. Purportedly more than 47 m high, these falls are only a few splashes short of the *other* Niagara Falls. Width and volume are a somewhat different matter.

3. Having taken your fill of photos, head downstream towards the highway. Immediately observe a rough track crossing the stream right above the tunnel and climbing precipitously up the bank on the other side. While your sense of adventure may compel you to take this route, you need not do so. The "official" trail is immediately next to the highway. Both these paths lead you to a small patch of old asphalt on the opposite bank.

4. Again, there are two routes. One narrow, rough track leads upstream along the edge of the gorge. The civilized route and official trail heads away from the stream; after a single large switchback it turns back to join the rougher route.

5. Head upstream on the broad, regular trail at the top of the gorge. The trail dips away from the stream and, protected by a section of chain-link fence, directs you back towards the stream and a pretty-enough little bridge, fairly close to the swirling waters above the falls. Reassuringly, the bridge is not only sturdy but criss-crossed with protective bands, largely eliminating the chances of a small creature plummeting into the dangerous waters.

6. Cross the bridge and begin the sequence of switchbacks through a stand of cedar and fir. When you come to a fork in the trail, keep right, but make a mental note of the other fork in case you want to extend your walk with a side trip down Gold Mine Trail (unsignposted here) after visiting the trestle.

7. Several routes are worn up the last few metres to the railway tracks. When the tracks are not being used, you needn't worry about a locomotive rushing towards you as you tread the airy heights of the impressive trestle. Checking, even with others who will almost certainly be there, will help. From the trestle itself, you have great views not only onto the treetops far below but also down the gorge towards Mt. Finlayson. (See *Popular Day Hikes 4: Vancouver Island* for directions on the hike up Mt. Finlayson.)

8. Returning the way you came, you may wish to explore along the clear, well-used trail to your right. If you follow it to the not-very-impressive vestiges of the historic gold mine, return the way you went: there is no good loop amongst these trails.

9. Once back to your car, you may well want to explore a little more of the park, particularly if you visit mid-fall for the chum salmon run. The Visitor Centre is also well worth a visit.

26. HORTH HILL

A low hill at the northern tip of the Saanich Peninsula in Horth Hill Regional Park, interlaced with winding trails amidst some attractive forest. Named after a pioneering family.

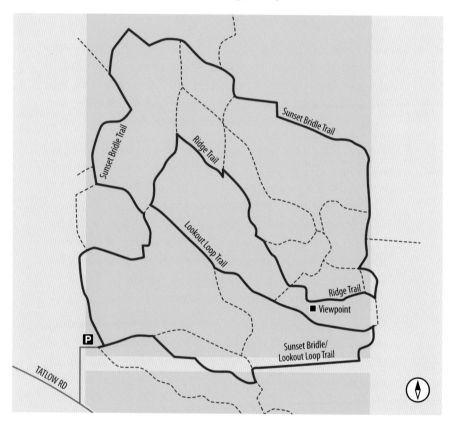

LOCATION

Driving on the Patricia Bay Highway (17) as you near the Swartz Bay Ferry Terminal, take the Wain Road exit (overpass). After about 600 m, turn right onto Tatlow Road and drive another 600 m, turning right at the large regional park sign. Drive the short distance to the parking area.

DISTANCE
3.2 km on suggested route, but many shorter options

ELEVATION GAIN
About 120 m cumulative (137 m if you go to the summit)

DIFFICULTY
Generally clear, even trails with a few rocky and rooty bits and moderate climbing. Main trails are well-marked.

SEASON
All season

OF SPECIAL INTEREST FOR CHILDREN
A spritely collection of inuksuks clusters beneath one of the rocky viewpoints, inviting a little further embellishment.

As you begin your walk, you may wish to have a look at the large map posted by the parking lot, but the one at the trailhead is much more accurate and detailed. The suggested wandering route here covers the greatest diversity of landscape and makes for the most substantial walk, but, as you see on the map, many shortcuts are possible.

---

1. Head right out of the parking lot, following arrows towards Sunset Bridle Trail and Lookout Loop Trail. The broad, largely level swath through cedars and firs can be muddy in the wet season, but it soon heads gradually uphill. Expect a narrower and drier path as it curves gradually to the left. When you come to the next signpost, take a sharp left to keep on the route for Sunset Bridle and Lookout Loop trails. Within a very short distance, however, take the right fork to keep on the same route.

2. As the trail traverses up the slope, you pass many fallen, mossy leviathans before coming to a split between the two trails you have had in mind until this point. Turn left

CLOCKWISE FROM LEFT Most trails contour through Douglas firs and sword ferns; the playful rock castles near the high point; licorice ferns and arbutus along the trail near the high point.

towards Lookout Loop Trail to contour along the south slope of the hill. When you pass an open area with a smooth, mossy outcropping, keep your eyes right to spot the gathering of inuksuks and rock castles at the base of a small cliff. Continue to contour on this trail, passing an informational sign and fork on your right. Descending slightly and entering the woods, to stay on Lookout Loop Trail, ignore a trail converging from the left.

3. Walk to a kind of T junction and turn right to begin the Ridge Trail sequence. Cross a low boardwalk and two minutes later come to a signpost pointing you on towards Ridge Trail and the viewpoint. Ignore a faint trail leading off to the left and climb quite steeply through a particularly lovely bit of forest, soon with the hill sloping down on your right. Pass another post pointing you ahead past a side trail on the left.

4. As you enter a zone of arbutus and licorice fern, slow down to saunter through the prettiest part of the trail towards the signposted viewpoint, ignoring yet another side trail to the left. Don't be discouraged that the trail begins to lose elevation slightly: you can see downhill on your right the information sign that you passed earlier on Lookout Loop Trail, confirming you need only keep ahead to reach not one but two adjoining viewpoints on Ridge Trail.

5. One of the viewpoints is additionally interesting because of its knobbly rock outcroppings. After drinking your fill of the views, and possibly having a refreshing drink from your supply, descend a short distance to an unsignposted T junction and turn left to arrive at a map, confirming that you are, indeed, at the beginning of (oddly named) Sunset Bridle Trail.

6. Your new trail – apparently little used by horses – leads you not towards but away from the sunset, around the east and north sides of the hill. Ignore the side trail to Hedgerow Drive. Pass some fine large cedars and a reassuring map confirming your progress. As you leave the cedars and move into a growth of comparatively small fir, watch for some amazingly tall arbutus. Ignore an unsignposted trail to the right and, a little later, a signposted trail to Willow Road.

7. On the final stretch of trail, you descend gradually, passing two more side trails, one to the right and one to the left. Welcome back to your car.

27. JOHN DEAN PARK

*Some of the most beautiful, varied forest walks in the
Victoria area, climbing around Mt. Newton to oak meadow
viewpoints and dipping into gullies of huge trees.*

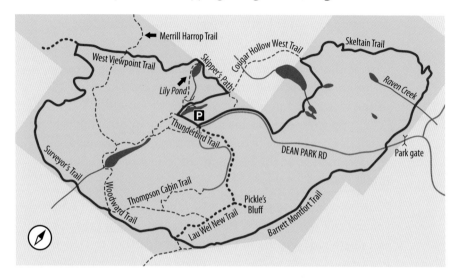

LOCATION
Driving north from downtown Victoria on the Patricia Bay
Highway (17), pass Elk Lake, and, just under 7 km later, turn
left onto Mount Newton Cross Road. Drive just under 1.5 km
and turn right onto East Saanich Road. After just under 3 km,
turn left onto Dean Park Road and go 2.8 km to the signposted
John Dean Provincial Park entrance. Park in the main parking
area at the end of the road.

DISTANCE
6.7-km loop (with shorter options)

ELEVATION GAIN
110 m, cumulative, over several short ascents and descents.

DIFFICULTY

Wide, even paths in some sections, narrow and a little rocky in others. Some sections are a little steep and rocky but safe for almost all walkers.

SEASON

Spring and summer. Unlike the regional and municipal parks in the area, this provincial park is closed to cars from November to mid-March. Theoretically, it is possible to walk in, but signs discourage parking on most surrounding roads. April and May are superb for wildflowers.

OF SPECIAL INTEREST FOR CHILDREN

A colourful sign with wildflowers could inspire a good treasure hunt in spring and early summer. At this writing, small (plastic!) creatures lurk in nooks along two sections of trail. One of these, the last section of Skeltain Trail on the suggested route, makes a fitting enticement to finish the long loop. The other is Thunderbird Trail, a suggested optional extra.

While many cross trails allow variations, the combination below provides lots of variety of terrain and offers the option of a long adventure.

---

1. From the parking area, walk straight ahead and to the right, downhill, past the outhouses and the sign for Valley Mist Trail. After a short drop, turn right onto a smaller trail. After zigzagging down a slope past some huge firs, go right past a cairn. Pause to study the colourful sign for wildflowers to add spice to your onward quest and swing right past a damp area to a signed junction.

2. Turn right onto Skipper's Path (also signed "Freeman King") and, in season, start looking for trilliums. Cross a small bridge with the puzzling sign saying "Rambling." At the next junction, ignore Bob Boyd's Climb, turning left to keep on Skipper's Path. Pass mostly cedars, sword ferns, of

course, blankets of salal and one of many particularly stately old firs. When you come to the sign for the old gazebo site, carry on past the so-called Lily Pond and up a double flight of wooden stairs, past Valley Mist Trail.

3. Now on West Viewpoint Trail, find yourself contouring and climbing into lighter forest. Pass a snag thick with bracket fungus, an impressively large mossy log and lots of Oregon grape. Go straight ahead at the junction (and posted map), ignoring Woodward Trail, leading off to the left. When you get to a small branch, you can either make a quick out-and-back trip along this narrow track to get something of the view it offers, or you can turn left onto Surveyor's Trail for your onward route and, as it happens, better views.

4. A striking formation of two large cedars and a fir deserves a photo at the very least. One of the huge, fire-scarred firs in the park also deserves a little attention and, possibly, some observations or reflections on the advantages of a thick skin! Descending to cross a tiny stone bridge, begin a climb until you pass another interesting old fir, this one (like others in the park) pocked by insect-hunting woodpeckers. When you reach signposted Cy's Lookout, and a beautiful bed of April-blooming fawn lilies, you are treated to lovely (though screened) views over Saanich Inlet.

5. Continue to climb gradually as the ecosystem changes and becomes increasingly dotted with arbutus, Garry oaks and grassy meadows. A side trail descending through a large meadow brings you to another viewpoint extending south to Brentwood Bay, unfortunately, close to a house. Fear not: in April and May, shooting stars and camas are beautiful distractions. Linger by these high meadows, for within minutes you find yourself switchbacking down to Canyon Creek.

6. Once across the strategically placed stepping stones of the tiny creek, climb quickly up a rough rock staircase of sorts and past junctions to Woodward and Thomson Cabin trails

CLOCKWISE FROM TOP One of many artful stream crossings, this one near Cougar Hollow; view of Saanich Inlet; a carpet of shooting stars in a meadow on the south side of the main ridge.

on your left. This second sequence of oak and arbutus meadows is almost as pretty as the first, but within a few minutes the trail begins to descend through small trees.

7. At the junction with Lau Wel New Trail you must make a major decision. While the recommended route lies straight ahead, you can cut the distance roughly in half by turning left here. Although this does shorten your walk, it does have the advantage of leading you close to Pickle's Bluff, a particularly popular

viewpoint. However, it takes you back to your car via some grim (but useful) structures at the high point of the mountain.

8. For the full loop, go straight ahead on the comparatively quiet Barrett Montfort Trail. This trail, contouring the mountain before gradually descending, has a feel to it quite unlike any of the other trails to this point. Narrow, but secure, the trail has something of a "real" mountain-trail quality, particularly as the bank steepens. With no junctions to think about, you can let your mind drift. Ultimately, the trail descends, levels out and brings you to the park road.

9. Climb the heavy-duty wooden staircase, cross the road and start straight ahead on "Barret" Montfort Trail West (Barret spelled here with one "t"). Pause at the inspiring sign with its photos of volunteers in the park before starting another section of contouring trail. More fire-scarred firs and more beds of fawn lily later, cross tiny Raven Creek and descend to the junction with Skeltain Trail.

10. Climbing along the sometimes-rocky path, come eventually to a mysterious junction with Cougar Hollow West Trail – mysterious because although signed, the trail (apparently outside the park) doesn't appear on park maps. In any case, turn left to stay on Skeltain Trail, dropping down dirt-and-timber steps. This last section of trail is a fitting conclusion to your trek. Particularly varied in terrain and rich with magnificent trees, it also has (or has had, perhaps) tiny plastic creatures lining its flanks.

11. Once on the paved road, turn right for the short stride back to the parking lot. When you are back at your car, you may feel inspired to visit the summit. One incentive for children might be to pass a second gauntlet of tiny plastic creatures, or, more likely, to stand atop the high point. But don't feel you are missing a wonderful experience if you opt out. Aside from a good view of Mt. Baker, you're not. See the comments in stage 7.

28. TOD INLET

A gently descending roadbed through moss-thick forest
above a rushing stream ending at an open picnic area
at the side of a small, deep inlet off Saanich Inlet
in Gowlland Tod Provincial Park.

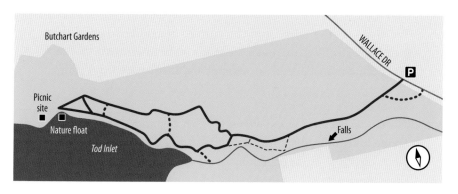

LOCATION

For the easiest but not the shortest route, drive away from Victoria on the Patricia Bay Highway (17) until you see the sign for Butchart Gardens and Keating Cross Road. Turn left and follow the signs, more or less straight ahead, almost to the Butchart Gardens (the road changes name to Benvenuto Road after crossing West Saanich Road). Turn left onto Wallace Drive and drive just under 500 m, until you see a yellow gate on the right-hand side of the road and a tiny sign for Gowlland Tod Provincial Park.

For the shortest route from the Patricia Bay Highway from Victoria, take Exit 11 onto Royal Oak Drive. Take the overpass left over the highway and, just under 1 km later, turn right onto West Saanich Road. After about 5.5 km, turn left onto Wallace Drive. After approximately 3 km, keep a weather eye open for the small Gowlland Tod sign on your left near a yellow gate.

DISTANCE
Approximately 3-km partial loop (depending on how much wandering you do near the end of the trail).

ELEVATION GAIN
55 m

DIFFICULTY
The slope is so gradual and the surface generally so good that even baby strollers can make the grade (in both senses!). The sections of ravine-side trail are steeper and involve (sturdy) stairs.

SEASON
Winter is best for good views of the rushing stream in the ravine and the eye-smacking brilliant green of the astounding moss displays. Summer is obviously the prettiest, particularly since in winter 2017 a lot of chewed-up earth was replanted for regrowth. The purple martin city of birdhouses atop pilings in the bay can be awhirl with occupants during the warm months.

OF SPECIAL INTEREST FOR CHILDREN
This is one of the few trails in the area that is suitable for kids on bikes – though keep in mind that the slope, barely noticeable on foot, can become more than just noticeable to little pedalling legs. The floating interpretive centre (not always open) and picnic area by the inlet can be much-hyped destinations.

1. Head through the gate, or, if you parked a little south, you can take an equally large track since the two quickly converge. Almost immediately you are immersed in a forest draped in deep, green moss. Adding to the mythic atmosphere is the colourful sign welcoming you to "traditional WSANEC territory" – or "Place of the Blue Grouse." Pass through some dense clusters of tall, mossy maple and fir and an odd, wire-fenced section of walkway. The monumental concrete ruins you pass next are only the first of many

CLOCKWISE FROM LEFT Remarkable growths of lichen along the trail; the rushing falls near the beginning of the trail are best viewed by stepping slightly off the trail; the nature float and, behind, a village of purple martin houses on pilings.

such traces of the former cement plant dotted throughout this part of the park.

2. Cross to the edge of the ravine for the best views of the rushing creek and get on the downward trail. Pass an intriguing cluster of cedar and enter a grove of comparatively small maple and alder. Do make a point of drawing your children's attention to some truly bizarre growths of green lichen, looking almost like oak trees from a fantasy landscape.

3. Almost immediately, find a newly planted garden on your left, the result of work to naturalize this area of concrete

ruins. Ignore the road on your right and, within a few steps, the one on the left heading downhill. As you approach the shoreside flats, you may want to wander and explore the various curiosities. Amongst other bits and pieces, notice that, through the chain-link fence, you can glimpse a fountain within the Butchart Gardens, in another area useful outhouses, and, along the side of the inlet, picnic tables. A visit to the little docks, to the floating nature centre (if it is open), to the information sign about the original First Nations village, and to a viewpoint on the purple martin houses are all good fun.

4. For the easiest, but not the most interesting, way back, simply retrace your route. For a little more excitement, keep near the water's edge as you head back, picking up a comparatively narrow trail. Ignore a cross trail; take a small bridge straight ahead. Contour upstream and descend a flight of timber-and-dirt steps. The trail straight ahead goes down to a bit of murky shore. To continue upstream, take the steps upwards on your left.

5. When you come to a railed viewpoint looking down on the small falls (worth at least a few photos), you have reached more or less the end of the maintained and passable part of the trail (at this writing). If you like that sort of thing, go straight ahead down the stairs to poke about the shards of historic broken pottery that have been collected and laid out before returning up the stairs and taking the broad trail away from the ravine.

6. Once back on the main trail, turn right and return to your vehicle, taking time to marvel at some of the tree formations you sailed by on your way to the inlet.

29. MT. WORK

*A varied trail in Mount Work Regional Park, up one
of the highest and most scenic hills in the Victoria area,
culminating in a long section of rocky ridge, dotted with
manzanita bushes and arbutus.*

LOCATION

While it is possible to climb the mountain
from Munn Road, the suggested route starts
at the opposite end of the mountain. Follow
the Patricia Bay Highway (17) from Victoria
and take the West Saanich Road exit. After
about 7 km, turn left onto Wallace Drive and
go about 0.5 km. Turn left onto Willis Point
Road to drive just under 4 km. Make a left
onto Ross Durrance Road, and a short distance along you can see a parking lot on your
left with a large map and signpost. Even in
winter this is a popular spot, so parking can
be difficult. There are signs forbidding parking along the adjoining "pavement" – but not
the unpaved broad shoulders.

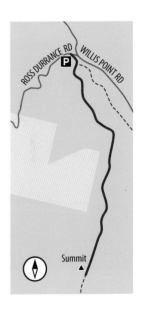

DISTANCE

4.8-km return (though the signs indicate more)

ELEVATION GAIN

310 m up to the 449-m summit

DIFFICULTY

Considering the length and altitude gain, don't make Mt. Work
your first family hill hike, particularly if you're not sure of your
charges' fitness levels and willingness to break into a sweat. The
trail itself is perfectly safe but does require a little clambering up
chunky rock and over fairly steep, rooty trail.

Arbutus, pines and weathered firs frame most of the views on the uppermost ridge.

SEASON
All season, but the usual advice applies about the possibility of encountering winter snow and chilly winds.

OF SPECIAL INTEREST FOR CHILDREN
The top section of the trail is marked with yellow and black signs pointing to the trail ahead. You may decide your child can be trusted to dart ahead to the next sign to await lumbering parents. The sections of bare rock towards the summit make an appealing challenge for mini-mountaineers. Then, of course, there is always the perfect picnic spot.

CLOCKWISE FROM LEFT The best views east are from spots just past the summit; along Saanich Inlet towards Bamberton and Salt Spring Island; the distinctive dome of Mt. Finlayson southwest of Mt. Work.

1. The first part of the trail resembles nothing so much as a road. Contouring around the mountain, it also functions as an access route for mountain bikers heading to the mare's nest of challenging trails on the east side of the mountain. Fork right onto the signposted trail to the summit, indicated to be 2.9 km distant (but is, in fact, less). The trail climbs steadily through open forest on a kind of spur off the north end of the long, ridge-like bulk of the mountain, at this point visible through the trees to the right.

2. Curving around to follow the spine of the mountain, the trail levels out in a grove of small fir and arbutus. Don't be

dismayed as the trail descends slightly: this ridge trail does that repeatedly along this section of the mountain. When you come to a kind of crossroads, notice the first of the yellow plaques with black arrows. These accompany you all the way to the summit. Ignore a side trail to the right as you come to another onward-pointing arrow and begin to climb more steeply over a rooty section of trail.

3. The next section of trail starts to take on a more adventurous feel as it switchbacks up a comparatively narrow bit of ridge, with the land dropping off steeply on either side. When you come to a viewpoint and, beyond it, an apparent descent, do pause for a few photos, but don't think you've reached the summit. Press on through the thickets of small fir and arbutus, rising and dropping along the ridge of the mountain.

4. Soon you come to an open area of rounded, mossy rock dotted with strange little manzanita bushes. Pause for some wonderful views towards Saanich Inlet and the Malahat. Ignore a side trail to the right by following the yellow marker to the left. Passing again into trees, soon find yourself climbing over irregular, lumpy rock and then, at last, arriving at a little plaque indicating the summit. Although you don't find much of a view here, the foreground of rock and ornamental-looking trees creates the impression of a lost-world rock garden. For the best views, carry on past the summit a short distance. The open area of exposed rock, descending in gradual steps, gives you impressive views past Mt. Finlayson to the far distant Strait of Juan de Fuca and the Olympic Mountains.

5. As you return the way you came in, more views than you thought were there on your way up will open before you.

30. LONE TREE HILL

Although no longer crowned by the original lone tree,
this exposed, rocky hilltop in Lone Tree Hill Regional Park,
at 364 m, is certainly not lacking in dramatically
poised lone trees or precipitous views.

LOCATION
From Highway 1, near Langford, turn
north on Millstream Road (towards the
Highlands) and drive for 8.1 km. The
signposted parking lot is on the right.

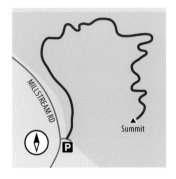

DISTANCE
2.3 km

ELEVATION GAIN
145 m

DIFFICULTY
Moderate, requiring a reasonable level of fitness and the ability
to clamber over some uneven rock surfaces.

SEASON
All year, but spring will allow the possibility of finding fawn lilies
and shooting stars, and, later, camas.

OF SPECIAL INTEREST FOR CHILDREN
This is one of those walks where the sense of standing on the
tippy-top, of being king or queen of the castle, can tap into
something primal and exhilarating for many kids. The quest
for turkey vultures hovering on the updrafts (except in winter
months) can be an additional boost. The summit area offers
many comfortable spots for laying out a treat-rich picnic.

FROM LEFT The nearly treeless summit of Lone Tree Hill allows for uninterrupted views; some small, steep sections of rock near the summit are great for mini-mountaineering.

1. Noting the presence of washrooms in the parking lot, start along the broad, ho-hum track running parallel to the road. Fortunately, within only a few minutes the well-engineered trail begins to climb through increasingly attractive vegetation and landforms. Like many of the hills in the area, Lone Tree Hill is shaped a little like the back of a whale. Thus, at first the trail switchbacks up the low end of the ridge-shaped hill. Almost immediately the trail dishes up pretty views through the scattered firs.

2. As the trail curves around to follow the spine of the whale, it runs through clefts, with the higher ground largely on your right. Passing some arabesques of arbutus, you have two opportunities to take short tracks to viewpoints over the refreshingly untouched-looking hills north and west of Lone Tree Hill. Peer at the highest close hill, Mt. Work, since you may want to tackle it (see Trip 29) if you haven't already done so.

One of many beautiful arbutus trees near the summit.

3. The last part of the walk takes you along the exposed bumps
    and lumps of the ridgetop, dotted with picturesque charac-
    ter trees. A kind of false summit, just before the real high
    point, might pose a bit of a challenge to wobbly little legs, so
    be careful. There are two routes over this bump, with no sig-
    nificant advantage of one over the other. The view from the
    top is as close to a full 360° as you find from any of the hills
    in the area. Most easily identified, in a direct line with the
    ridge axis, is the prominent dome shape of Mt. Finlayson
    (see *Popular Day Hikes 4: Vancouver Island*).

4. Return the way you came.

31. BEAR HILL

A little visited, but easily climbed, hill in Bear Hill Regional Park
near Elk Lake, with wandering trails through open character
forest to views over the north end of the Saanich Peninsula.

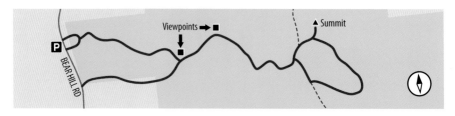

LOCATION

Driving north on the Patricia Bay Highway (17) towards Sidney, turn left onto Sayward Road and drive just over 100 m. Continue along Hamsterley Road for another 100 m, and turn right onto Brookleigh Road. After 2.4 km, turn right onto Oldfield Road and drive 1.2 km until you come to Bear Hill Road. (Be careful as you drive along Brookleigh Road, since you may notice a sign for Bear Hill Road on your right. This section of Bear Hill Road does not connect with the north section where the park entrance is located – though a trail connects the two sections of the road.) Turn right and drive just over 1 km (watch for the right crook to keep on Bear Hill Road). The signposted gravel parking lot is on the left.

DISTANCE

1.8-km partly return, with two small loops

ELEVATION GAIN

150 m

DIFFICULTY

Apart from the perils of puffing and stumbling over some patches of rough trail, this is a compact, only moderately challenging, little-hill climb.

SEASON

All season, though April is best for wildflowers.

OF SPECIAL INTEREST FOR CHILDREN

Children will have to be content with the delights of an easily gained hilltop that gives the special sense of feeling on top of the world. The fact that the rounded summit is a perfect picnic spot will not, of course, go unnoticed.

1. Do not proceed to the trailhead next to the small parking area, but do note this as your destination. For now, walk a short distance along the road to start along the alternative trail. Don't be put off by the dour sign: "Warning. Steep Trail. Loose Gravel." Most intrepid families will find this to be a mild exaggeration. In fact, this bit of trail is open to horse riding (though little used by horses). Wandering through firs, arbutus and Oregon grape, the trail climbs stolidly to a lovely, open area of rounded mossy rock. You see the original trail you spied in the parking lot (your way down) converging from the left. Even this low spot will reward you with some fragments of distant views.

2. Encounter one of the roughest parts of the trail now. Handle this, and you can handle anything on the whole circuit. When the trail levels out, watch for two small side tracks to the left – at least, if you want to nab more pretty views. The next bit of trail is lovely in a different way, as it swings to the right, wandering gently along a terrace beneath oaks and through licorice ferns.

3. Come to a junction with a large signpost, noting that you will return to this spot via the trail pointing to Brookleigh Road. For now, though, take a deep breath and turn onto the left branch towards the signposted summit. With the summit in sight ahead, turn right to follow a second sign labelled "Summit." Pass a trail on your right (you do come back to this junction), and whip out your binoculars, camera

CLOCKWISE FROM TOP LEFT Looking north towards Sidney; large arbutus and firs along the trail; Overlooking Saanich farms towards James Island and Sidney Island.

and energy bars. For, yes, you have reached your destination – excellent views of James Island, Sidney Island and Mt. Baker in one direction, and, in the other, Saanich Inlet.

4. Tear yourself away from the view to return the few steps to the broad trail, now on your left, heading into scattered arbutus and oaks. Pass a small trail to the left (though it does provide yet more view) to swing consistently to the right. When you come to a T junction, turn right and, within no distance, find yourself back at the junction with the large summit signpost.

5. Retrace your route down the mountain to the open mossy area where the two upward trails first converge. This time, turn right to swing around below this open area. As you approach the road and your vehicle, there is a split in the trail. Worry not – both trails will take you back to your familymobile.

32. ELK/BEAVER LAKE

*Level, groomed trails past Elk/Beaver Lake Regional Park
facilities, beaches and through some old forests, with the option
of shorter loops and a 10-km loop of the two linked lakes. As for
the puzzling double name, the southern bulge happens to be
called Beaver Lake and the northern, larger bulge Elk Lake.*

LOCATION

Drive north on the Patricia
Bay Highway (17) towards
Sidney. Both the entrance to
Elk Lake and Elk Lake itself
are prominently visible. Traffic lights and a dedicated left-
turn lane make turning off
the busy highway easy. Once
in the park, drive through
the first parking lot to enter
the forest. Drive along the
narrow park road to Beaver
Beach. Park where you see
an obvious beachy area with
lawns and, on the right, a
Nature House.

DISTANCE

4 km

ELEVATION GAIN

Insignificant

DIFFICULTY

Probably the easiest walk in
the Victoria area, not only
because of the level, groomed

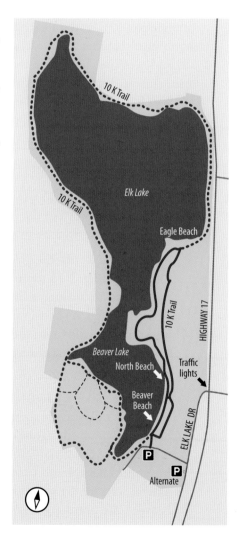

trails but also because of the many facilities and the options for taking shortcuts.

SEASON

All season, though, of course, to take advantage of the water, summer is best.

OF SPECIAL INTEREST FOR CHILDREN

With one of the warmest beaches in the Victoria area as the culmination of a loop walk, this trip's appeal is obvious. (Blue-green algal blooms have occasionally precipitated swimming advisories.) When it is open, the Nature House is good fun. It is open June to September, weekends and holiday Mondays, from noon to four. When all else fails, the playground is a sure bet for children.

There are dozens of shortcuts – and extensions – possible. The loop described here begins and ends by a beach and provides some of the prettiest views and greatest variety. Directions here are simplified because the trails are so well-signposted.

---

1. Walk first towards the beach to eye it speculatively for future dabbling. Turn towards the Nature House and, if it is open, consider making a little visit. Pick up the broad trail by the lakeside. A partial screen of willows on the left and a forest of large, old fir on the right quickly embrace you with a restorative sense of nature at its most reassuring.

2. When you come to a small cross trail and a picnic bench at North Beach, have a look at the map and take the smaller, shoreside trail with the signpost directing you towards Eagle Beach. At the next signpost, the trail converges for a few metres with the official "10 K" loop trail, which runs around the entire lake system. Turn left to take the shoreside alternative. Some of the prettiest views, past the small island in Beaver Lake, are along this section.

CLOCKWISE FROM ABOVE Much of the trail along Beaver Lake is behind a lattice of trees and bushes; the lakeside trail is almost entirely level and wide; near the beginning of the trail along Beaver Lake; the broad "10 K" trail often leaves the lakeside to run through large trees.

3. The trail cuts across a peninsula before curving around the base of another bay, with a potentially welcome park bench. At the next junction, assess the energy of your intrepid group, since this is a good place to turn away from the lake and make a shortcut back to the starting point. Otherwise, complete the north end of your loop by continuing along the shoreside walk until, nearing Eagle Beach, you swing inland to a T junction.

4. If you are curious about the home of Canada's rowing team, turn left and walk a few minutes towards Eagle Beach and the Victory Rowing Society's boathouse before turning back to this point. The fairly direct route back to your starting point is along the well-signposted 10 K trail, also signed for Beaver Beach. If you are set for the 10-km circuit, this is a good place not to turn right but left, away from your starting point. The loop will be a little more than the official 10 km because of the shoreside route you followed until this point, but it's well worth the additional steps.

5. On your way back to your vehicle, pass several side trails, all of them well-signposted. Simply keep ahead on 10 K trail. Although this route is away from the water, it does lead through some soaring and soulful large forest. At several points, too, if you yearn to get back to the shore trail (and avoid the slight hill on the 10 K route) you have plenty of opportunity to follow side trails a short distance to the shore.

33. STEWART MOUNTAIN

A hidden and little-visited gem just north of Thetis Lake in Thetis Lake Regional Park, this hill has lovely mossy bluffs, arbutus groves and sweet views towards Victoria and Sidney.

LOCATION

Heading north from Victoria on Highway 1, turn right at the major intersection signposted for Millstream Road. Pass the shopping centres and, after 5 km, turn right onto Stewart Mountain Road. Drive to the end of the road, a

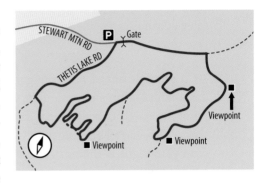

little under 2 km along. Park where you see a gate blocking further progress and where you see a gravel track on the right with a regional district sign saying "Stewart Mountain Road."

DISTANCE
2.8 km (full loop)

ELEVATION GAIN
110 m (271-m high point)

DIFFICULTY
The narrow trail climbs steadily over some rocks and roots, but it requires no scrambling. The optional loop, switching to comparatively small and unsignposted mountain-biking trails, requires some route finding. The regular shape of the mountain, lack of obscuring bushes and presence of clear landmarks prevent you from becoming (very) disoriented.

SEASON
All season, but obviously mid-spring is best for the chances of wildflowers.

OF SPECIAL INTEREST FOR CHILDREN
Some of the rounded rocky outcroppings by the summit are appealing for some king-of-the-castle/dirty-rascal moments. Turkey vultures can sometimes be seen hovering on the updrafts (in summer).

1. Go straight ahead past the gate and along a broad gravel road until, after a few minutes, shortly after a sign announcing the Thetis Lake Regional Park regulations, you notice an established trail heading uphill on your right. The land rising on your right is the northwest flank of Stewart Mountain. Note the location of the large power lines ahead since they are a useful means of orienting yourself if, instead of returning the way you came, you descend the long way through mountain-biking switchbacks.

2. The trail climbs steadily, very quickly bringing you to a zone of arbutus and open fir forest with lovely beds of undulating moss. When you come to a junction with a trail on your left, follow it a short distance to your first viewpoint. While the large hydro lines may be charmless, the distant views aren't. Return to the main trail and turn left, uphill.

3. Find yourself walking along the long axis of the ridge, with rocky bluffs on your right. Come to one particularly impressive old Douglas fir, scorched by the flames of a historical fire. When you emerge from the trees onto a rounded, mossy high point, you see a well-travelled side trail heading south to Scafe Hill (231 m) and, in the far distance, central Victoria.

4. The simplest way back, of course, is to retrace your route, but for a bit of adventure and the opportunities for exploring some beautiful terrain, take the trail heading off the south end of the ridge. Almost immediately this trail starts

CLOCKWISE FROM TOP LEFT The view from the bluffs and the south end of the ridge; one of many grand old character firs on the mountain; the view looking towards Thetis Lake from the summit; there are many beautiful, large arbutus along the main ridge.

swerving to the right. Don't be misled. The mountain-biking trails here make several long loops along the terraced steps, dropping gradually down this side of the oval-shaped hill. Use a small set of power lines (not the large ones at the other, north end of the ridge) as your landmark for this generally untreed south end of the hill. The first switchback is the largest, taking you almost to the north end of the ridge and the main Stewart Mountain Trail before swinging back and undulating via short switchbacks towards the south end.

5. At the south end, with the open bluffs and small power lines visible ahead, the switchbacks are so close together that you may feel understandably tempted to take the trail connecting the ends of the switchbacks. A clear trail winds down to the gravel road that leads towards Thetis Lake. Turn right when you reach this road to climb slightly and walk the few minutes back to your vehicle.

34. FRANCIS/KING REGIONAL PARK

A tree hugger's paradise! A maze of diverse and carefully signposted trails over knolls and, above all, through gorgeous old trees. The park is named after Thomas Samuel Francis, who donated most of the land that makes up the park, and famous Vancouver Island naturalist Freeman "Skipper" King – hence the oblique in the park's name.

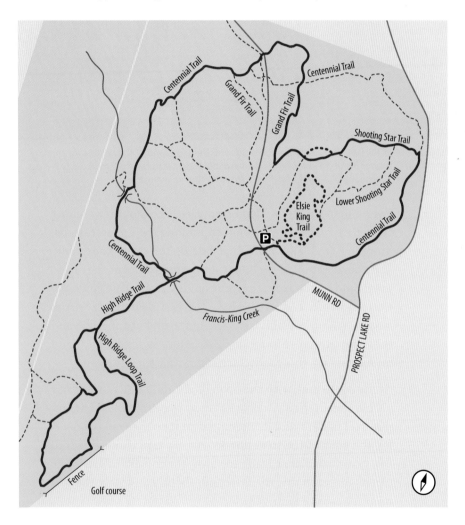

LOCATION
From Highway 1, heading north from Victoria, take Exit 10 for Burnside Road West. After just under 1.5 km turn left onto Prospect Lake Road and drive 1.2 km. Turn left onto Munn Road and drive 0.5 km. The large Capital Regional District sign for the park is on your right.

DISTANCE
3.4-km loop, plus 1.8-km loop

ELEVATION GAIN
70 m

DIFFICULTY
Mostly easy to moderate, though with some narrow, rooty sections and some noticeable rises, and, seasonally, large muddy sections to wind around.

SEASON
All season, though late spring is best for possibilities of spotting wildflowers, especially on the ridge loop.

OF SPECIAL INTEREST FOR CHILDREN
The 800-m Elsie King loop, along deluxe pathways, can be a good preparation for the longer loops. Absorb some of the natural history from the colourful and colourfully worded signs, and prepare, as a team, to apply that knowledge to finding, for example, "tree's knees" and "nurse stumps." The nearby nature centre is open from 12:00 to 4:00 p.m. on weekends and holiday Mondays. For those taking the High Ridge option, llama-spotting is a surprising and delightful possibility!

While several variations are possible through the maze, the suggested route hits many of the best features.

FROM LEFT The trail begins in a particularly bright and open section of firs; All intersections in the complex network of trails are clearly signposted.

1. Find the trailhead for Centennial Trail tucked between the two buildings to your right. The least inspiring part of the whole circuit is the first stretch of narrow trail, largely parallel to the road. Most appealing are little patches of licorice fern and Oregon grape and the increasingly cliffy, moss-covered rocks rising above the trail.

2. Arriving at the signpost for the connector to Shooting Star Trail, turn left to climb up a rocky crest on the narrow, winding trail. When, after a significant climb, you get to the signpost and fork, turn right. The trail takes its name, unsurprisingly, from the striking pink flowers that bloom in early April. This next part of the trail is largely level, under open, established forest with some stately old firs. Look for the blackened burn scars on one impressive specimen just before descending to the junction with Lower Shooting Star Trail. Keep ahead, though, when you reach the junction with Skunk Cabbage Loop, you may wish to take this alternative if you arrive in spring (or even summer).

3. Continuing your descent past a snag with bracket fungus, follow signs via a connector trail to Grand Fir Trail. Turn right to walk a low, damp section of land through probably the best stand of grand fir on any park trail in the lower part of Vancouver Island.

4. When, however, you get to a bit of unsignposted trail leading to a cross trail, rejoin Centennial Trail and turn left.

Climb up and over a pretty, little mossy knoll and, within a short distance, turn left to cross Munn Road. Go straight ahead on Centennial Trail. As the trail curves gradually to the left, pass two side trails simply labelled "Parking Lot." Between the two, the smaller members of your expedition should be thrilled to discover a little cave. Be glad you brought your camera.

5. As you drop into lower and damper ground, notice the increasing number of moisture-loving cedars. One of these, shortly after the second connector trail to the parking lot, is particularly striking for its partially rotted trunk and many woodpecker holes. At the junction with the third Parking Lot trail, turn sharply to the right to cross a low bridge and a seasonal mud-o-rama.

6. From here the trail takes on a new aspect, since the uphill slope is now on your right. At the next signposted junction, you have a decision to make: trot the 370 m back to the parking lot, or sally forth onto High Ridge Trail. In making your decision, don't be misled by the name. The trail is not very high, nor is the "ridge" much more than a generally raised area of rounded mossy knolls. The views are almost entirely of trees rather than distant vistas. On the other hand, the woods along the route are probably the prettiest in the park.

7. Assuming you are going to go the whole hog, begin your new adventure by crossing a little bridge and, in winter, navigating your way through a bit of a muddy mess. Take heart. You soon begin the gradual climb along lovely trail to the fork leading to High Ridge Loop Trail. For now, turn right to walk the loop counter-clockwise. Be pleased that you chose to come here as you walk through what many would consider the prettiest part of the whole trail system.

8. After a deep bend around a pond, the trail comes to a T junction. Mystifyingly (at least in terms of the official park map),

FROM LEFT Battle-scarred old fir demonstrates charring from a fire; Moss and cedar boughs can create a magic pattern.

both right and left are High Ridge Loop Trail. Turn left to begin the last phase of the loop. Pass over an enchanting mossy crest and, shortly after, some especially masterly old firs. Ignore a signposted trail on the right pointing to Thetis Lake Park (though keep the spot in mind for other possible adventures in route finding).

9. Brace yourself for a bit of a shock as you come to a fence and vehement Private Property signs keeping you from trespassing onto the groomed lawns of a golf course. After winding back and forth along this barrier, come to a charming little farm with – usually visible – llamas! Heading back to complete the ridge loop takes you past an intriguing woodpecker-pitted fir almost directly on the trail.

10. Navigating your way back across the mud, and regaining Centennial Trail, turn right to pass some boardwalks and ascend through the open stands of cedar to the beginning. Don't be in such a rush, however, that you miss one of the last delights of this part of the trail: the multi-trunked Six Sisters cedar just off the right of the trail.

35. MILLSTREAM CREEK TRAIL

Although crowded at some points by houses, this trail is one of the easiest wooded walks in the Victoria area and one of the only ones where very little children can bring their bicycles.

LOCATION

Driving north on Highway 1, as you pass Thetis Lake and approach Langford, take Exit 14 towards Langford/Highlands. Drive along Millstream Road for about 1.3 km until you come to Goldie Avenue. (Be aware there is another section of Goldie Avenue, off Bellamy Road, not contiguous with this one.) Drive to the end and park – considerately – in the cul-de-sac.

DISTANCE

1.6-km return

ELEVATION GAIN

10 m

DIFFICULTY

Vies with Langford Lake and Elk Lake as being the easiest trail in the area. Level, groomed and well-signposted, it could hardly be easier.

SEASON

By far the most attractive when the leafy bushes screen nearby houses along some sections of the trail. The creek largely dries up in summer.

OF SPECIAL INTEREST FOR CHILDREN

The possibility of small children being on bicycles and stopping to explore a trailside playground are the chief draws. Two footbridges over the creek and some bizarrely shaped trees are interesting features. The creek itself is too dark and muddy to be of much interest. In August and September, expect some tempting blackberries near the trailheads.

1. Walk through the blackberry patch and cross the odd little metal footbridge over the willow-screened creek. Turn right along the trail, past a fine thicket of salmonberry, to enter the forest, mostly of cedars. This first section of the trail features some amazingly twisted cedar trees, once perched atop nurse stumps, now with their roots perilously suspended. This is the perfect spot for a little edifying question-and-answer session with curious children.

2. When you emerge at the end of a paved road (the other end of Goldie Avenue), your children may feel a scientific investigation of the little fenced playground, visible to the left, is required. Clearly indicated with white posts, the trail re-enters the forest. Pass contorted trees before coming to probably the most interesting feature of the trail, a long, wooden footbridge, complete with arched entranceway. The still waters of the creek can make for lovely reflections of the overhanging trees.

3. Once across the bridge, you must run the gauntlet of an uninspiring bit of trail along residential fencing, though some of it is quite well-screened. Buttressed by concrete and separated from the steep drop by a handrail, the trail passes some lovely large trees before descending slightly and passing a bit of rushing water.

4. Emerging from the trees to run parallel to a schoolyard, the trail brings you to a patch of blackberry bushes and Treanor Avenue. Cross the avenue and pass beneath some grand firs along the largely creekside trail. The trail comes to an

CLOCKWISE FROM LEFT Several fantastically formed cedars line the first part of the trail.; the carefully crafted bridge is one of the main features of the walk; a large cottonwood and sample of the smooth, even trail.

unprepossessing end on Selwyn Road (a short distance from Millstream Village, but not easily accessible from here).

5. Return the way you came.

Optional Add-On: Connections to Florence Lake Trail and Strachan Trail
It is possible to design a longer route by using a combination of roads and trails to connect to nearby Florence Lake Trail and Strachan Trail. See the City of Langford website for details of this longer route.

36. MILL HILL

One of the prettiest and most easily accessible of Victoria's hills, complete with Garry oak meadows, spring flowers and views, views, views. Housing developments are creeping like mould up Mill Hill, but, blessedly, from most viewpoints, they don't interfere with your experience of this lovely bit of wilderness in a sea of burbs.

LOCATION
Off Highway 1, near Langford, take the ramp towards Sooke and drive 0.8 km to Hoffman Avenue. Turn left. After 100 m, turn right onto Winster Road, drive for 160 m and go left again onto Atkins Avenue. Drive for 1 km, and, as you enter a stand of fir, pass the entrance to the Capital Regional District offices and, immediately afterwards, the large sign for the entrance to Mill Hill Regional Park.

DISTANCE
1.7-km loop (seems like more!)

ELEVATION GAIN
120 m

DIFFICULTY
There is a huff-and-puff factor, but the trail to the summit is mostly smooth and regular. The descent, via eroded Calypso Trail, can be challenging at a few spots for those with weak knees or short legs. An out-and-back walk is probably best for such walkers.

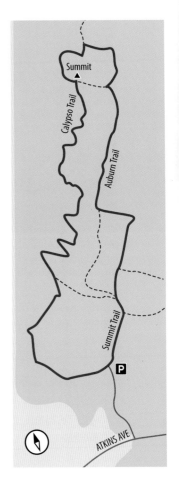

The upper meadows and knolls are thick with wildflowers in the spring

SEASON

All season, but April is the very best, both because the wet sections will have shrunk and the sea blush, camas and so on will be at their flowery finest. Remember, as with any hill, if there is even a sprinkling of snow or a light breeze at the bottom, life can be noticeably chillier at the top.

OF SPECIAL INTEREST FOR CHILDREN

For children who like the experience of being at the tippy-top, this hill has the double appeal of having a good 360° view and a circular plaque naming distant points. Rounded lumps of rock make perfect snacking perches.

1. Straight ahead out of the parking lot, pass information signs and a signpost. Head more or less straight up the broad, crushed-gravel Summit Trail and, next, Auburn Trail,

ignoring side trails (Calypso Trail and, a little later, Millwoods Trail) on your right. Take time to appreciate some of the large Douglas firs and cedars, because within a very short distance you suddenly emerge into a completely different ecosystem.

2. Within minutes, notice the sign about the Garry oak ecosystem you are entering. This sign advises you to stay on trails to protect the ecosystem. Along this section of trail, you see only a few stunted and windblown Douglas firs, as well as arbutus and Garry oaks. The rounded rocky outcroppings are decorated with mosses, licorice root ferns and stonecrop. All is not well in paradise, though – expect to see lots of invasive species as well: broom, daphne and, a little more charmingly, large bounding grey squirrels. (On the bright side, volunteer "broom busters" have made it possible for the native vegetation to emerge, gasping, from under former thickets of broom.)

3. Passing some split-cedar fencing, turn right onto the viewpoint trail (ignoring the trail for the summit). From here, the views to Portage Inlet, Esquimalt Harbour and the distant Olympic Mountains are, let's face it, little short of exquisite. If you've printed out a regional park map from the web showing the viewpoint trail to be a dead end, ignore it. Walk past the viewpoint on a well-trodden trail at some points lined with rocks.

4. Within minutes, reach a major trail labelled both "Summit Trail" and "Calypso Trail." Turn right for only a few steps before branching off to the left to climb up to the rounded hump of the actual summit. From the summit you not only have a 360° view but also see an impressive cairn mounted with a brass info-wheel, indicating the exact direction and altitude of visible bumps – ranging from Race Rocks, a mere bump in the ocean, to Mt. Baker, 120 km distant and 3261 m high.

5. Passing over the hump and coming to a junction with concrete stepping stones beside a small pond (dry in summer),

FROM LEFT Esquimalt Harbour and downtown Victoria from near the summit; one of many patches of shooting stars in April.

turn right down a small trail. Be warned, however: if you have small and/or (endearingly) clumsy children, you are best off going straight ahead to rejoin the trail you used to climb the hill. Otherwise, be prepared for a little rough walking and head down the small trail. In spring (especially April), have both your camera and your *Oohs* and *ahhs* ready, since this trail descends through some gorgeous spreads of wildflowers.

6. Though not dangerous, the heavily eroded trail does require a little care, even hands, as you descend some step-like chunks of rock.

7. With almost no transition zone, the trail plunges into heavy forest. Several switchbacks later, you pass a trail leading to your left. Forge straight ahead to visit some of the largest Douglas firs in the park (while ignoring the regional district offices increasingly visible ahead). Cross a small asphalt road to pick up the final bit of trail.

37. MT. DOUGLAS

*The most iconic and popular hill in the Victoria area,
and deservedly so. Magnificent forest at the bottom of the hill,
a large network of trails and a wide range of views from
the top make for a great family destination.*

LOCATION

From just about anywhere in Victoria, find your way to Shelbourne Street, a main thoroughfare running north–south. Drive to the north end. As you enter large forest, the parking lot for Mount Douglas Park is prominently signposted on your left.

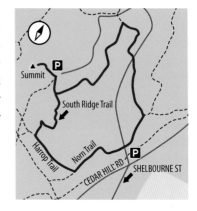

DISTANCE

4-km loop

ELEVATION GAIN

205 m (altitude: 225 m)

DIFFICULTY

An easy and popular route to the top is simply along the paved road. The suggested route for older children, more isolated, adventurous – and attractive – involves a little route finding and some clambering up bits of fairly steep, rocky trail.

SEASON

All season

OF SPECIAL INTEREST FOR CHILDREN

Several labelled "wildlife trees" can intrigue curious children with eyes tuned to spotting flickers, pileated woodpeckers and downy woodpeckers. Specially selected, too, is this adventure route for those children who love a sense of achievement in the (controlled) outdoors.

The paved road to the top is closed to traffic until noon each day and can be used, therefore, as a kind of all-purpose trail during the morning for those who want the easiest walk to the top. Because the hill is so popular and is so intertwined with improvised trails, particularly near the summit and the south end, keep in mind that no two the of many maps are the same. Fortunately, plentiful signposts make route finding comparatively easy.

---

1. From the parking area (complete, note, with a portable biffy), and facing uphill, turn right onto Norn Trail. Whether or not the trail is named after the Norse mythological figures who rule destiny, there is a mythic atmosphere surrounding the winding, level path through large cedars. When you come to a signpost, switch your destiny to Irvine Trail, heading sharply to the left. Walk gradually uphill through a section of split-cedar fencing and past two much-pecked wildlife trees. If you feel like engaging in a little edification about forest fires, pause and comment as you pass a venerable, fire-scarred Douglas fir.

2. When you reach the paved road, you can pause at the bench before picking up Irvine Trail slightly to the right and across the road. If you're wondering why the trail symbol changes from a blue square to a black diamond, remember that the latter is supposed to signify "difficult." Point this out to children who are eager to sniff out adventure. The trail does, indeed, become a little steeper climbing past the fir forest and into a zone of Garry oak and licorice fern. Make your way up a slightly challenging knoll of exposed rock and, at a junction, fork left to continue on Irvine Trail unless, reconsidering, you turn right onto the paved Churchill Drive.

3. The next section, partly through large firs and arbutus, rises in stages, at some points beneath fairy-tale bluffs of licorice

CLOCKWISE FROM TOP LEFT Downtown Victoria backed by the Olympic range; Sidney and D'Arcy islands framed by weathered firs; the distinctive banks of James Island and the San Juan Islands behind.

fern. Watch for small, foot-level "Irvine" signs to reassure yourself, particularly as you pass increasingly frequent side trails and make your way over some narrow, rocky bits of steep trail. Although the trail is never dangerous, you may want to keep stumbly children close to you at some sections. At others, be prepared to heft them up steep rock steps. Along this section you get some good views over Cordova Bay, many of them framed by Garry oaks.

4. As you near the top of the hill, you must find your way through a maze of user-made trails, most of them to viewpoints. You can't really become disoriented because looming over you is the transmitter tower near the top. Turn up towards this tower when you reach an unsignposted T junction by a forked arbutus below the tower. Alternatively, you can keep contouring around the mountain to get some more views before turning up on a convenient trail to the tower.

If you come to the South Ridge Trail sign, turn back to make your way up to the tower to avoid too much repetition, since you will be coming down South Ridge Trail.

5. Approaching the tower, come to a broad trail descending to the summit parking lot, a view terrace and, no doubt, photo-snapping throngs. Join them, certainly, but also certainly take the paved trail across the parking lot to the highest point. Enjoy some of the best views in the whole Victoria area, particularly of downtown Victoria backed by Mt. Olympus and, in the other direction, the Gulf and San Juan islands.

6. Retrace your route towards the tower, but as you approach it, fork right onto signposted South Ridge Trail. Any feeling of insufficient adventure to this point just might shift on this new trail. Two options, an easier and a rockier one, bring you to what is clearly a ridgetop stroll and the beginning of the trail proper. Thereafter the trail starts to drop down natural rock steps, well-signed to prevent unpleasant consequences from straying off the safe route. Brace your troops for a minor thrill as you descend to what appears to be a promontory surrounded by vertiginous cliffs. This, of course, is an illusion. The perfectly safe trail swings right and drops by more steep, rocky steps towards the forest.

7. Switchbacking left and passing a section of split-cedar fencing, the trail passes through groves of Garry oak and brings you to a T junction. A signpost announces this to be the end of South Ridge Trail and points both left and right to Harrop Trail. Turn left to follow the fenced trail down into the fir forest. When you come to an unsignposted fork, turn left. Pass a large fire-scarred fir, and keep left when an unsignposted small trail heads off right.

8. When you reach the signpost indicating the end of Harrop Trail, turn left onto Norn Trail (sound familiar?) and follow it – via a wildlife tree and a boardwalk – back to your starting point.

38. LANGFORD LAKE/ED NIXON TRAIL

Though surrounded by suburbs, an amazingly untouched bit of old forest alongside a lake and its opportunities for fishing, picnicking and swimming.

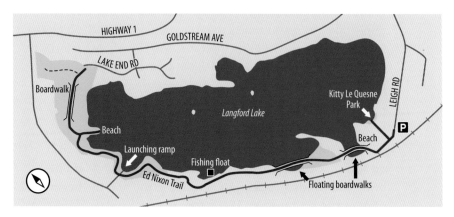

LOCATION

Driving north on Highway 1, as you pass Langford, take the signposted Leigh Road exit (the overpass crosses the highway). Drive just over 1 km along Leigh Road. Turn right onto Leigh Place and drive for 500 m. The sign for Langford Lake Beach Park parking is on the left.

DISTANCE

4.6-km return

ELEVATION GAIN

Negligible

DIFFICULTY

Could hardly be easier. Smooth gravel path and boardwalks, with only a few gentle undulations.

SEASON

All season

OF SPECIAL INTEREST FOR CHILDREN

This is a bit of a kid's paradise, particularly in warm weather. The swimming spots are plentiful, the trail is great for riding bicycles and the lake is stocked with rainbow trout for angling. There is even a local population of painted turtles.

1. Walk left along the road, passing a sign for Kitty Le Quesne Family Park. If you are curious, you might pop down the short distance of this smooth gravel path to the lakefront, where there is a small floating dock and pleasant view. Since there is no connection with Ed Nixon Trail, however, you probably just want to bypass this trail to arrive at Langford Lake Park. Here you find a little sandy beach, picnic tables, a playground and washrooms (though be alert to the warning signs about potential issues with algae if you're toting bathing suits). Notice a walkway to an alternate parking lot on Langford Parkway.

2. Pass along a few metres of asphalt road to start along signposted Ed Nixon Trail. Cross the lovely boardwalk to begin the trail, and, a short distance beyond, enter a kind of willow bower. If you're lucky, for the next several minutes, you walk through not only this amazing growth of dense willows but equally amazing cascades of redwing blackbird song. You also pass the first of several distance posts (this one 0.25 km) that dot the whole trail.

3. Cross another, longer section of suspended boardwalk, this one too with a midpoint viewing platform. The next section of the trail introduces you to some of the grand old trees that line much of the rest of the trail. While you are aware of being close to considerable development along the left side of the trail, leafy bushes (except in winter) generally provide a good screen. In any case, for most of the rest of the trail, a high bank and broader width of forest give a soul-refreshing sense of being in genuine forest, far away from what is, in fact, not far away. Lots of invasive minor players – primarily

CLOCKWISE FROM ABOVE One of many low bluffs around the lake favoured by photographers and fishermen; floating dock popular with anglers; a view from above of the impressive walkway and unusual shoreline near the beginning of the walk; the southeast end of the lake.

daphne and holly – have little impact on preventing nature from doing what she does so well.

4. Arrive at a little floating platform and, if you have rod in hand, a good opportunity for pursuing the wily trout. Continue winding your way through some fine old grand firs, Douglas firs, cedars and even arbutus. Pass a slightly elevated viewpoint. As you circle around the north end of the lake, notice a sign warning you of a track crossing the trail and leading to a boat-launching ramp. Go down to the shore for a colourful sign about the painted turtles in the lake.

5. Back on the main track, you come to a fork in the trail. For now, ignore the gabled entrance to a long boardwalk. Instead, turn right to arrive, after a short distance, at an excellent viewpoint, swimming beach and picnicking spot.

6. Return to the main trail and turn right to come to the last – and wonderfully distinct – section of the route. An astoundingly long, elevated boardwalk takes you through the largest growth of hardhack – a pink, flowering bush – that you are likely to find anywhere. Arrive in early to mid-summer to find the pink flowers at their most resplendent.

7. Once across the boardwalk, note a white signpost for Henson Trail and a little along to the right, a plaque on a stone for Ed Nixon, after whom the trail to this point is named. Although it is possible to circle the lake by walking the obvious route along roads, by far the prettier option is to return the way you came. If you do decide to walk along the roads, be aware that Lake End Road, the first road you come to, ends in a cul de sac. Turn up, therefore, to Goldstream Avenue, and follow it to Leigh Road, following the route you drove to start the walk.

39. MT. WELLS

Feeling like a proper, rugged (little) mountain,
Mt. Wells, with its double summits, is best suited
to those wanting more than just a gentle walk.

LOCATION
Follow the Trans-Canada Highway from Victoria towards Sooke, and turn left onto West Shore Parkway. After driving for 400 m, turn right onto Amy Road and go 800 m before turning left onto Sooke Lake Road. Drive for 350 m and turn left onto Humpback Road and drive for about 1.5 km. (Be careful. When you come to Irwin Road, stay right.) The signposted Mount Wells Regional Park entrance is on the right.

DISTANCE
2.6-km return

ELEVATION GAIN
240 m; climb up to 352 m altitude

DIFFICULTY
Moderately difficult, though those who are sure-of-foot, and in fine fettle, will not be fazed by either the somewhat slippery and rough rock surfaces at some points or the elevation gain.

SEASON
All season, though there are a few muddy bits in winter, and, of course, if there is a little snow at the bottom in winter, there will be more at the top. Look for camas lilies in late April and early May.

OF SPECIAL INTEREST FOR CHILDREN
Even more than most other hills in the area, Mt. Wells can stir up those Sir Edmund Hillary self-images. At the base of the mountain, a small section of the Sooke Flowline can allow children to sample

FROM ABOVE Weathered trees near the summit indicate how strongly winds can blow here; the view towards the Malahat and the resevoir. Chain handrails make walking over the exposed rock comfortable.

what could, on another venture, become a major outing. As for the picnic opportunities at either summit, well, enough said.

1. You may wish to look at the colourful signage before starting up the trail by the parking lot. First, climb the wooden steps over the fragment of this former waterline. The temptation is understandably strong to walk a short distance along the top of this concrete pipe (although the practice is not officially encouraged). Some adventure seekers walk along many kilometres of the long-distance pipeline. This first part of the trail is just an approach to the main mountain trail, as you see when you come to Humpback Road. Cross the road and walk via a second section of pipeline to wooden stairs and the proper trailhead.

2. Pass the sign saying "Warning. Steep Trail. Loose Gravel." – and be glad you are wearing proper footwear and are reasonably sporty. The trail doesn't waste any time in starting uphill, zigzagging and offering two equally good routes to a bit of a ridge, thick with lush moss. A little farther along, the irregular rock formations, heavy with moss beneath writhing arbutus, invite evocations of popular fantasy epics.

3. The atmosphere changes significantly as the trail drops into a salal-thick gully before beginning a series of switchbacks. With each leg to the left longer than the corresponding leg to the right, the trail goes increasingly into the forest until coming to a small trail leading to the left. A large Capital Regional District park sign saves the day: follow the trail to the right and towards the summit.

4. This is where the drama begins. Traversing to the right and climbing steeply, the trail delivers you to a bit of rope-assisted scrambling (with no precipitous drops to spoil the fun). As you emerge from the trees onto a moss-covered slope, a system of metal chains and posts keeps you to the straight and narrow, as much to protect the fragile vegetation as to assist you. Follow this fence to the left, over

FROM LEFT Victoria Harbour viewed from near the summit; the summit is a garden of rock and weathered arbutus.

sections of gravel and exposed rock, to arrive at the false summit. Even from this high point, the sense of height created by the steep slopes, and the views both towards Esquimalt and the Malahat make this a good turnaround spot for those who are worried about biting off a little too much.

5. Bound for the true summit? Follow little blue markers across the flat, mossy area to descend steeply into a gully. Passing some especially picturesque arbutus, the trail climbs out of the gully and, after a small drop, begins crossing over the ridge so that, soon, the high ground is to the right. After wandering through a fir grove, the trail emerges to fine views towards Esquimalt. Now approaching the largely treeless summit, the trail, dotted with small blue markers, wiggles its way through fragile ground cover to the high point. Manzanita bushes and a few beautifully weathered firs and arbutus pose for dozens of photo possibilities.

6. The return route is the same as the outbound route. Be careful, though, as you stand thoughtfully on the high point, not to follow your nose back along the summit ridge. Doing so will get you to some small cliffs. Instead, therefore, swing back the way you came to follow the marked route back to the trees and the clearly designated trail.

40. DEVONIAN REGIONAL PARK

Winding through characteristically windblown Metchosin forest, the trail arrives at the long sweep of Taylor Beach, before returning to the parking lot via open, rocky knolls.

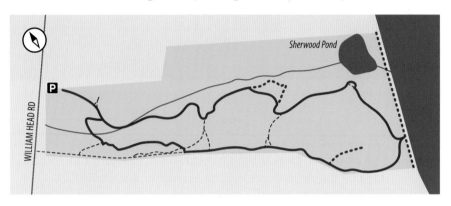

LOCATION

Driving north away from Victoria on Highway 1, turn off at the Langford/Millstream Road exit. Cross over the highway to enter Langford. After 5.5 km, continue straight ahead along Veterans Memorial Parkway (Highway 14). Approaching 6 km, turn left onto Latoria Road. At the T junction with Metchosin Road, 1.8 km along, turn right and drive along Metchosin Road. After 5.2 km, passing Metchosin Store, the road changes name to William Head Road. Drive for just over 1.6 km and pull into the well-signposted parking lot on your left.

DISTANCE

1.9-km loop, plus beach walking

ELEVATION GAIN

50 m, mostly on return leg

DIFFICULTY

Easy, well-graded and well-signposted park trails. Some muddy sections in winter. A few rocky bits on return loop.

CLOCKWISE FROM LEFT Licorice ferns and exposed oak meadows on the bluffs near the ocean; a blaze of colour from sea blush in the oak meadows; the sea bluffs are particularly dense with camas in the spring.

SEASON

All season, but spring is best for wildflowers on the rocky knolls by the Garry oaks.

OF SPECIAL INTEREST FOR CHILDREN

The beach, with its opportunity for log walking, stone skipping and creating soggy havoc, is the most obvious feature. The principle of The Picnic, of course, underlies any *reasonable* visit to a beach.

1. After passing by – or visiting – the toilet, march purposefully into the fine stand of trees, noticing as you approach them how the howling offshore Metchosin winds have deformed the oldest Douglas firs. Follow the signpost to Taylor Beach, for now ignoring the right branch to Helgesen Bridle Trail. Drop down a slope to cross a natty little footbridge over Sherwood Creek and climb slightly for the next few minutes until you come to a junction. Both the trail leading up past timber steps on the right and that on the left, leading slightly downhill, converge after a short distance, though the left branch is probably a little more interesting since it skirts marshland. Climbing significantly onto a kind of ridge over stone steps, the trail passes some rock-garden-like patches of licorice fern and stonecrop.

2. Descend timber steps and pass beneath a steep bluff of arbutus and Garry oak before emerging onto Taylor Beach. Unless you arrive at low tide, you encounter a long, sweeping pebble beach. No doubt you will want to walk some distance along the log-lined shore before returning to the park.

3. Turning off the beach past the large park sign, begin the return leg of your walk by climbing up a sparsely treed, rocky knoll. The trail winds through perhaps the prettiest part of the whole loop before approaching the heavy forest. Beyond the wire fence that demarcates the edge of the park, farm meadows remind you of the pastoral nature of most of Metchosin.

4. Now on the bridle trail, ignore a signposted branch trail to the beach on your right. When you come to the third branching trail on the right, descend slightly below the bridle trail to traverse alongside a heavily treed slope. This trail curves to follow the contours of the slope before dropping down to Sherwood Creek.

5. Cross a well-constructed little bridge and climb some timber-and-soil steps to complete the loop and arrive back at the outbound trail.

41. MT. MANUEL QUIMPER

Old rutted roads in Mount Manuel Quimper Regional Park, climbing to rock-and-moss bluffs dotted with weathered trees and beautiful views extending from Victoria to Sooke Basin and the Olympic Mountains.

LOCATION

Driving towards Sooke on Highway 1, note the prominent junction to Gillespie Road. About 4 km later, passing Saseenos and Ayum Creek, turn right onto Harbourview Road. Drive the short distance to the end of the road in the gated and signposted Mount Manuel Quimper Regional Park.

DISTANCE

10.5-km partial loop (or 8.5-km direct return)

ELEVATION GAIN

480 m (546-m high point)

DIFFICULTY

This is at the most challenging end of the family-hike spectrum because of the altitude gained, the total length and some rough or steep sections. Families with fairly small children, however, regularly reach the summit.

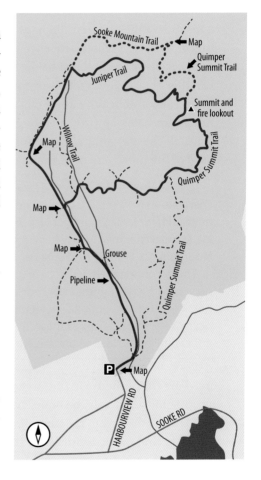

SEASON

All season, but one section can be very wet. Remember, especially an issue in winter, the top will be 3–4°C cooler than the base and exposed to wind.

OF SPECIAL INTEREST FOR CHILDREN

Some children will respond well to being given this significant challenge – some not. The fire lookout station at the summit will appeal to some children. Perhaps placed there strategically by cagey parents, a whole sequence of small plastic animals lines one section of the trail just below the false summit (who knows whether they will migrate – or multiply!). Older children with strong legs and healthy lungs might feel motivated to ride their mountain bikes up (the operative word) the logging road that leads all the way around the mountain to the outhouses at the base of the north end of the summit trail.

There are many similar routes in the Sooke Hills. Many of these are quite long for families and not well marked. Those who have enjoyed Mt. Manuel Quimper, however, might consider exploring Monument Mountain, Mt. Braden, the Sugarloaf, Empress Mountain and others.

The recommended route here strikes a balance between easy gravel road; broad, rutted track; and narrow, picturesque trail. It is possible, at some optional points indicated in the description, to decrease or increase any of these. Be aware, though, that a few trails appearing on the map as options are for mountain bikes only.

---

1. Pass the outhouse in the large parking lot and turn uphill on the logging road. The branch on the right leads to a narrow trail all the way to the summit. However, for a comparatively easy and quick approach to the base of the mountain, the gravel road to the left is best. Running parallel to a gurgling stream, the road leads steadily uphill past a trail on the left. Pause when you come to the old concrete pipeline accessible on both sides of the road. It could be fun to assess what walking along this now-derelict, long-distance flowline

Sooke Harbour and East Sooke from near the summit.

would be like. (Although hiking along the pipeline is officially discouraged, doing so has become quite popular.)

2. Continue ahead past a posted map and Grouse Mountain Biking Trail, as the road swings away from the stream and brings you to a set of side trails and a second map on your left. Keep ahead on the gravel road under the shade of trees until you come to a third posted map and a broad, newly gravelled trail on your right called the Quimper Connector.

3. Take the Quimper Connector. Ignore a little-travelled track on the right and, shortly after, pass a signposted roadbed (Willow Trail) on your left. Cross a spanking-new, sturdy metal bridge, and begin to climb an increasingly rutted track through small firs. As you pass signed Raven Trail on your left (a one-way downhill trail for mountain bikes only), the Quimper Connector becomes narrower and more heavily eroded.

4. Pass by a signposted second approach to Raven and Arbutus trails and begin a significantly gentler part of the connector. Passing the signposted Manzanita Trail on the right, the connector soon turns into a section of old corduroy track (notice the old cross logs). Sometimes very wet, this section ends at a pond and, within minutes, brings you to a T junction with Summit Trail.

5. Turn left and begin a steady climb through scrub trees until, eventually, you emerge in an open area dense with broom. As you enter this area, be sure to swivel around for lovely views of Sooke Basin and the Olympic Mountains. Climbing steadily over exposed rock up a largely treeless slope, the trail suddenly appears to be visited by strange little (plastic) creatures peering at you from the side. How long they have been there or will be there is uncertain, of course, but if your timing is right, they may be a real incentive for children with flagging enthusiasm.

6. After reaching a kind of false summit, the trail dips through a hollow, and crosses through a thicket of small lodgepole pine, manzanita and kinnikinnick before swinging sharply left. This corner is usually marked with flagging tape. This last phase of the climb is unquestionably the most attractive. The narrow, switchbacking trail contours along and up grassy slopes with several character firs and increasingly mouth-watering views. This is camera time! The signposted junction with Arbutus Trail points to the summit and the historic fire lookout.

7. Completing your visit to the tower, you must decide whether to save a couple of kilometres by returning the way you came or to go straight ahead for more adventure. Assuming the latter, descend over brows of rock and scattered trees, pausing when you come to a splendid view of Mt. Baker. Within a few steps, you are at another junction and must make another decision. The most common route involves

FROM LEFT Mt. Baker looms above Sooke Hills from a viewpoint near the summit; the trail near the summit.

going straight ahead down Summit Trail to a T junction, an outhouse and the gravel road that leads back to the parking lot. Much prettier, however no longer the recommended route down, is Juniper Trail. Although primarily a mountain-biking trail, it is open to walkers and is almost never busy. Winding down mossy bluffs through small firs, the trail occasionally drops into little thickets of salal before rising over more crests and swinging around more small bluffs, many with lodgepole pines (but nary a juniper). There are occasional splits in the trail, but these are all short side tracks that rejoin the main onward trail. The end of Juniper Trail at a T junction is accompanied by a posted map. Turn left down this broad gravel road. A stroll through some lovely forest will bring you to the junction with the Quimper Connector. From here to your car, it is all downhill!

42. BROOM HILL

A sometimes rough, user-made trail through large wind-gnarled firs to a splendid viewpoint over Sooke Harbour and East Sooke from an elevation of 283 m.

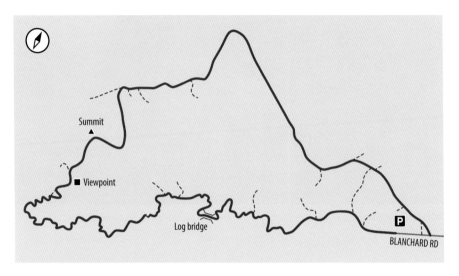

LOCATION
From the centre of Sooke (on Highway 14), turn away from the ocean onto Otter Point Road. After 1.6 km, turn left onto Burr Road. After one block, turn left onto Petemar Road. One block along, turn right onto Blanchard Road, and drive the short distance to the end of the road. Parking is limited at the end of the road, but the shoulder is wide enough to fit several carefully jockeyed cars.

DISTANCE
3.8 km

ELEVATION GAIN
180 m

DIFFICULTY

Overall, the trail is not very steep, but it is generally narrow and, in several spots, does require clambering up rock "steps," but with no dangerous drops. At two points it is necessary to walk along logs, though the logs have a good surface and there is no danger of falling very far.

SEASON

All season, though, in winter, if there is a little snow at the bottom, there will be more at the top.

OF SPECIAL INTEREST FOR CHILDREN

Suited for older, nimble children, the whole trail can be hyped as a bit of an adventure, with occasional obstacles. Also fun is a little swing rigged up near the summit.

Although there are many small trails criss-crossing the mountain, all unsignposted, the main trail up the mountain is, in most places, noticeably more travelled than the side trails.

---

1. Walk straight ahead up a broad, level track through salmon-berry thickets, passing a car wreck and taking the first fork left. Walk along a low log bridge over a damp spot, and begin to ascend by curving up around mossy rocks towards small fir.

2. Swinging left at the next fork through the salal, the trail levels out a little through sparse firs and arbutus before entering denser forest. Ignore a small trail to the right to climb a little over a mossy knoll and past a remarkable suspended mossy log. Think: brontosaurus neck and head! Wind up gradually over some more mossy knolls, this time noticing that the larger trail swings right at a junction with a smaller trail forking back downhill.

3. The next section continues to take you gradually uphill over a series of similar rounded, mossy steps. Within a couple of

CLOCKWISE FROM TOP LEFT Sooke and East Sooke from near the summit; the hill is remarkable for the number of character firs; one of the groves of arbutus near the summit.

minutes, ignore a smaller trail forking right through a cleft to swing left on the main trail, which brings you to your first real bit of adventure hiking! Walking along the log through the salal mats is good fun, not least of all because it is low to the ground. Also a little adventurous is the climb up the bluff immediately afterwards, again safe but fun. Add to this the first of a series of huge, old, wind-gnarled firs, and you're on your way to the most enjoyable part of the trek.

4. Ignore a small branch to the right and crouch-walk under a large fallen log across the trail. There is another small trail, with a yellow ribbon, converging from your left as you make your way around the side of the hill and past two amazingly fire-scarred old firs. Immediately after, the main trail swings

right past a small fork on the left through an increasingly rock-garden-like setting.

5. Pass pretty groves of arbutus and a mossy rock wall on your left as you catch glimpses of Sooke Basin downhill on your left. Within minutes, you have your first full-on views towards East Sooke and, beyond, the Olympic Mountains. From a little higher up you can also see back towards Sooke Basin – though your little ones might be distracted by the great swing rigged up next to the summit! Just about the only sign you see on the whole route points towards the unmistakeable summit a few steps along past small criss-crossing trails.

6. Crossing the high point over mossy stone, the trail heads roughly back towards your starting point, dropping quickly and easily down a broad path, at one point taking you between two large cedars. This part of the route, bordered with small logs and rocks, makes for particularly easy, fast striding.

7. After descending over some lovely sections of mossy rock, the trail joins a broad track. On the lower slopes, the wide trail leads smoothly through sword ferns and large cedars. A small path converges from the right shortly before the increasingly eroded trail heads more directly downhill through scrubby trees. Ignore a fork to the right to continue on the wide, now-rocky track, but go right at the next junction, and, within a very short distance, left (though the right fork will take you home too).

8. In the wet season, brace yourself for some huge puddles, though in all cases, a rough path through the bushes allows you a way around. Minutes before the end of the trail, taking the left fork will bring you out to Blanchard Road and a short walk from your vehicle. Congratulations! You've navigated your way through an adventurescape!

43. PEDEN LAKE

*A clear trail climbing through mixed forest parallel
to a small stream and concluding at a wilderness
lake with two good access points.*

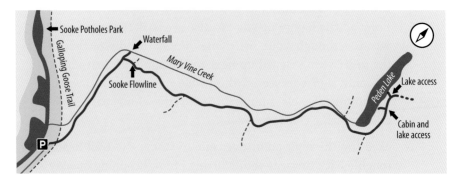

LOCATION
Approaching Sooke or leaving Sooke along Sooke Road, turn towards the prominently signposted route towards Sooke Potholes Park. Drive along Sooke River Road for 5 km to the park and (this is important) farther along to the last in the sequence of parking lots for the park. (In summer, be prepared to buy a parking pass.)

DISTANCE
5.4-km return

ELEVATION GAIN
225 m, mostly continuous with a few crests and dips en route.

DIFFICULTY
Mostly well-packed dirt trail with a few steep and rocky sections. Some wet spots in winter and spring.

SEASON
Tiny Mary Vine Creek (and its sets of waterfalls) is prettiest in the wet season, since it dries in summer. Spring is best for

FROM LEFT The waterfall on Mary Vine Creek; Peden Lake from the research cabin, a popular picnic spot.

wildflowers; summer, of course, for swimming. Accessible more or less all year, but there are a few muddy bits in winter.

OF SPECIAL INTEREST FOR CHILDREN

The lake at the end – with easy entry into the water – is the obvious magnet. Don't forget the chocolate chip cookies – there are good picnic spots.

1. After you check out the washrooms in the parking lot, take the broad path at the top end of the uppermost parking lot to Galloping Goose Regional Trail. Immediately across this broad gravel track is an unsignposted old roadbed, angling off gradually uphill. This easy introduction to your walk allows you to get into your stride for several hundred metres. Except when it's dry, Mary Vine Creek, bordered by salmonberry bushes, gurgles along below and parallel to the path. Angling away from the stream, and dropping a little through a patch of cedar, the now narrower trail begins to ascend more steeply and become a proper hiking trail.

2. Climbing onto a relatively open mossy area, pass (spring-blooming) fawn lilies and come to a clear side trail leading a short distance to a charming little waterfall and, of course, lots of photo ops. From here the trail swings away from the

creek, bringing you, after few minutes of fairly steep hoofing, to a large concrete pipe. The Sooke Flowline once enabled Victorians to fill their teapots and baths with water from Sooke Lake. Those who enjoy a long trek along the top of the waterline (an acquired taste) often begin their jaunt here.

3. After you ascend a gentle bluff, the trail comes to a T junction. Turn left to begin a bit of a roller-coaster section of sometimes-steep trail. Amongst other pleasures of this section are some fine, biggish firs and, at the top of an exposed bluff, a wonderful little manzanita grove. From this bluff, the trail drops to a potentially wet bit and an improvised bridge. Now in earshot of the gurgling stream, climb a little until you see a side trail to the left. Except in a dry summer, you can take a short side trip to a pretty little waterfall before continuing your adventure.

4. When you come to a pool or its dried bed, you see a trail blocked with branches and the much-more-used main trail swinging left and traversing up a slope. Within minutes the trail levels out, having joined an old roadbed for a little – but not for long. In fact, with the slope dropping off fairly steeply to the stream below and the trail becoming quite rocky, a few cautioning words to scampering children might be appropriate.

5. Pass next a striking giant boulder before dipping close to the stream for a short section and once again climbing and swinging away. At this point you are getting close to the lake and soon will have glimpses of the marshy end. Pass a minor but enticing viewpoint and come to a fork. Ignore the comparatively minor trail on the right and keep ahead close to the lake.

6. At the next junction, however, in a broad mud patch, look for a trail on the left leaving the main onward trail. A little vague for the first few metres, this trail soon becomes a major route to what is, in fact, probably the most popular spot on this side of the lake. Here is a little unlocked green

The rope swing and view from the second access spot.

cabin with a sign saying "Research Cabin" – not very enticing, but it can make a good emergency shelter. The views
from the open area of rock and moss on the edge of the lake,
though, are a satisfying climax of your walk – unless you
decide to go just a little bit farther along the main path to
a second rocky viewpoint. The trail to this spot begins as an
indistinct scramble over a small ridge of rock. A favourite
dipping and picnicking spot, this second destination also
sports an impressively engineered rope swing for those who
like to take an adrenalin-fuelled plunge.

7. It is possible to go farther along the edge of the lake (and
    indeed, connect with a whole maze of trails), but, in the
    absence of other close lake-access spots, it makes sense to
    turn around here.

44. SANDBAR TRAIL

A well-designed trail winding through forest, along a riverbank, and ending at a gravel bar with thickets of dune grass and pretty views across deep river pools.

LOCATION

From the tourist information building at the entrance to Port Renfrew, start down West Coast Road towards Sooke. After just over 1 km, where the highway swings right, turn sharply left onto Red Creek Main (a bumpy logging road) and drive a short distance to a rough T junction. Park on the side of the road where you see the Sandbar Trail sign.

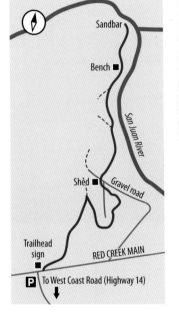

DISTANCE

1.6-km return

ELEVATION GAIN

Negligible

DIFFICULTY

Generally level, smooth going, usually thick with needles and moss. At this writing, one patch of deadfall and one short, uneven section are the only real challenges.

SEASON

All season

OF SPECIAL INTEREST FOR CHILDREN

While the trail has its charms, most children will perk up only when the sandbar is in sight, not least of all because this is a great spot to break out the provisions.

Fantasy bench near the end of the trail.

1. The trail begins auspiciously with a second (weather-beaten) trail sign and the first piece of flagging tape marking most of the route. The easygoing romp almost immediately grinds to a halt by a hefty mess of deadfall – though, with luck, you may find the way through has been cleared.

2. Once past the deadfall, the sword-fern bordered trail curves prettily away from the road through moss-festooned forest. Within minutes the narrow trail joins a level, much-faded roadbed. Coming to a junction where you can glimpse, to the right, the moss-covered hulk of a blue pickup, turn sharply right to join a cross track.

3. Walk parallel to a small (barely visible) gravel road on your left and find yourself heading back in the direction of Red Creek Main. Panic not. The trail soon turns sharply left around the head of this small dead-end road, and then runs roughly parallel to its opposite side. This is the only section of trail where the ground can be a little uneven underfoot. It is also probably the best area to spot the wary trillium in early April.

The river flows gently past the sandbar.

4. When you pop out of the woods onto this gravel road, turn right for a short distance – but only a short distance. Pass a shed on your left and, instead of following the gravel road to the right, go straight ahead onto the flagged trail leading enticingly back into forest.

5. Soon be aware of a river on the right, just out of view. Ignore a broad track leading to the left, and whip out your camera for the highlight section of the walk. The trail runs along the edge of the smooth-flowing river (a branch of the San Juan) for a short section, dips into the woods and re-emerges beside a spectacularly fantasy-inspired bench. You might have to supervise wobbly little legs for a few metres along the next bit of eroded trail.

6. Dipping away from the river, this particularly attractive section of trail brings you within minutes to the famous sandbar. Since the river is tidal – not to mention susceptible to winter flooding – the size of the gravelly area varies considerably. Nearly always, though, there is more than enough space here to spread out your bits and pieces and soak in the quiet.

7. Return, refreshed, the way you came.

45. DEAKIN & BEAUSCHESNE TRAIL

Taking its name from the pioneer families who homesteaded here, this generally pleasant route through moss-hung second-growth forest becomes a prime destination during the pink fawn-lily bloom in the latter part of April.

LOCATION

From the tourist informa-tion office at the entrance to Port Renfrew, drive along Deering Road, cross-ing a small bridge, and, after 1.4 km, turn right at a fork and go another 1.4 km until you reach Deer-ing Bridge. Once across the bridge, turn left onto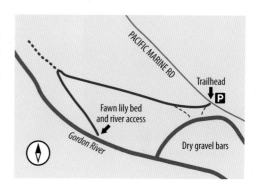
Gordon River Main (unevenly paved). Just over 6.5 km from Port Renfrew and about 1.5 km past the sign for the marina, look for a wide gravel track dropping down from the shoulder of the road. Visible from the road but several metres away is a sign on a tree saying "Trail."

DISTANCE

1.5-km return

ELEVATION GAIN

Negligible

DIFFICULTY

Level, smooth roadbed.

SEASON

All season, but the wet season produces some large puddles. These can be skirted with a little effort. Mid- to late April

The beginning of the trail.

transforms a pleasant outing into a magical experience with a carpet of pink fawn lilies beside the fast-flowing river.

OF SPECIAL INTEREST FOR CHILDREN

This is one of the only trails in the area where small children can pump furiously along on their bikes while parents stroll. The riverbank is a little bouldery but still makes a good spot for getting up to no good in the water.

1. Descend the broad gravel track. Instead of going straight ahead onto a gravel bar, turn sharply right past a sign prohibiting motor vehicles and up a small embankment to the grassy track marked with a Trail sign. Notice strips of flagging tape, though they are not necessary along the obvious trail and, at this writing – be warned – farther along lead into thickets of bush (though a route through may be cleared to the old homesites when you visit).

2. Enter the woods over a carpet of false lily-of-the-valley with their heart-shaped leaves. You soon see a broad dirt track

FROM LEFT The Gordon River from the end of the trail; thick with moss.

merging from your left. Join this old roadbed. Walk straight ahead between hedges of salmonberry and beneath the strange forest of nearly identical, moss-heavy fir.

3. When you come to a broad track merging from the left, turn sharply left. Within a few minutes, emerge from the forest and, in season, find yourself in a sea of pink fawn lilies. The short drop to the broad riverbank of the Gordon River is easy and worth making, even if you do nothing more than stroll to the edge of the river for the views up- and downstream.

4. Return to the first junction and turn right to retrace your route back to the beginning. If, however, you wish to extend your walk a little, instead of turning right go straight ahead onto the pleasant track heading upstream. Access to the river along this section, however, is not good and even while strolling ahead you soon find yourself climbing around and over clusters of deadfall. When you've had enough, swivel in your tracks and head back to the starting point.

46. AVATAR GROVE/T'L'OQWXWAT

"Avatar Grove" is the English nickname, inspired by the movie of the same name. The traditional name is "T'l'oqwxwat" in the Nuu-cha-nulth Pacheedaht language. This is one of the premier short hikes on Vancouver Island. A series of staircases and walkways leads up and down a steep hill amongst remarkably large – and remarkably shaped – old-growth forest, primarily, but not exclusively, cedar.

LOCATION

From the travellers' information centre at the entrance to Port Renfrew, drive along Deering Road, crossing a small bridge, and, after 1.4 km, turn right at a fork and go another 1.4 km until you reach Deering Bridge. Once across the bridge, turn left onto Gordon River Main (unevenly paved). When you come to a fork about 5 km along, go left and cross a bridge over a breathtaking gorge. Keep on for about 1.5 km, swinging right at the next fork. The road can be rough going but is usually passable with all but the lowest-slung cars. Within minutes, when you cross a small bridge, park beside the road and look for the prominent signs.

DISTANCE

3-km part return, part loop

ELEVATION GAIN

95 m, cumulative

DIFFICULTY

Partly on boardwalks and wooden staircases, with anti-slip surfaces, all the more impressive because these were built by volunteers of the Ancient Forest Alliance. BC Parks, take note! Those with walking difficulties should be aware that the staircases have no handrails for support: bring your walking poles. Seems to involve more climbing and descending than it actually does.

SEASON
All season, but, even with all the boardwalks, expect to get wet feet in the wet season unless you are appropriately shod.

OF SPECIAL INTEREST FOR CHILDREN
Only the most video game–desensitized child will not get something of a thrill out of the twisted giants and adventure-playground stairs.

As you see from the sign, the trail is in two sections, one on the lower side of the road, one – with "Canada's gnarliest tree" – on the upper side.

---

1. Assuming you wish to see the most-touted tree first, head left up two steep staircases. From here to the gnarliest tree, appropriately at the end of the ascent, there is no ambiguity in the route. In some places you must climb over exposed networks of roots, pick your way over boulders or tread carefully over (potentially slippery) rounds of log. En route you pass several fascinating giants, presumably spared from logging because of their awkward location on the side of a ravine and because of their unprofitable burls and twists. You cross one small stream shortly before arriving at the roped-off base of the flagship tree: help to protect the tree by respecting the barriers.

2. Returning to the road, start on the lower trail by descending a few stairs to an airy viewing platform. From there, continue to a split in the path. Turn left to follow a boardwalk snaking horizontally through second-growth hemlocks, sword ferns and deer ferns. On this part of the loop, a section of boardwalk allows you to cuddle up close to a burl-encrusted cedar and a grand old Douglas fir before coming to the brink of a ravine.

FROM LEFT The so-called gnarliest tree in Canada – a huge, old cedar; another gnarly giant, this one on the lower trail; impressive staircases and boardwalks run past dozens of giant trees.

3. The trail curves right to follow the edge of the steep slope running parallel to the Gordon River, far below and barely visible. Pass a sketchy descending trail as you wind on mostly dirt trail through several character trees, some having managed to survive being suspended above nurse stumps.

4. Once you have closed the loop, you see a boardwalk leading sharply to the left. Take this boardwalk to climb a little. The narrow trail traverses around the end of a kind of tributary gorge. Pass a steeply descending, rough trail to finish your discoveries with a couple of mighty old trees and the last of the gnarly cedars.

5. From here, it is probably best to return the way you came to the junction of trails, and ascend to your vehicle via the viewing platform. (It is possible to continue on a very rough trail up to the road, but this user-made route is a bit of a tangle of branches and logs.)

47. FAIRY LAKE NATURE TRAIL

A mossy, lush wander amongst large second-growth hemlocks and spruce, leading to the banks of a clear-watered creek.

LOCATION

From the information centre at the entrance to Port Renfrew, drive across the bridge onto Deering Road. About 3 km from your start, cross another bridge. At the T junction, turn right onto Pacific Marine Road – the paved route to Cowichan Lake. About 2.5 km later, on your right, look for a small sign and a broad shoulder where you can park. Potentially useful landmarks are a logging road branching off to the left just west and off the trailhead and, visible ahead, a blue and white road sign.

DISTANCE
2-km return

ELEVATION GAIN
Negligible

DIFFICULTY
Generally, very easy, though, depending on recent maintenance, you may have to step over the occasional fallen tree.

SEASON
All season, since the trail is blessedly free of puddles and mud, even in winter. Early April is trillium time! The creek can be virtually dry at the end of a hot summer.

OF SPECIAL INTEREST FOR CHILDREN
While the creek at the turnaround spot is appealing and easily reached, probably the biggest attraction is a menagerie of tiny

CLOCKWISE FROM LEFT Much of the moss-heavy forest has a primeval atmosphere; lovely little Fairy Creek dries at the end of a long summer; large spruce and sword ferns on a typical part of the trail.

plastic critters perched along the trail on mossy stumps (though it might be best not to set expectations high in case they have wandered away by the time you visit). The creek bank makes a good picnic spot.

1. The little-used trail is narrow and mossy. Keep your eyes open for pink flagging tape marking the route, more for reassurance than for any real need. The trail wanders and winds gradually to your left on the outbound trip. You pass plenty of huge, old stumps, often surrounded by huckleberry and salmonberry bushes. The forest floor is beautifully carpeted with false lily-of-the-valley, sword ferns and deer ferns.

2. When you come to the shores of beautiful Fairy Creek, you must scramble down a couple of steps. It is possible to wade across the stream and make your way, on the other side, to Fairy Lake. Since, however, the trail is not a loop, you must either walk back to your car along the road or come back this way. Probably best, therefore, to return the way you came and drive the short distance to Fairy Lake and its recreational treats. Break out the fishing rods and bathing suits.

48. LIZARD LAKE NATURE TRAIL

A looping forest trail around a pretty wilderness lake.

LOCATION

From Port Renfrew, drive towards Cowichan Lake on Pacific Marine Road. About 18 km from Port Renfrew, the sign-posted Lizard Lake Rec-reation Area is on the right side of the road. Three different exits from the highway lead to

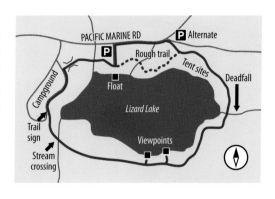

different parts of the campground. The second one, by a floating dock, is the best starting spot for your walk.

DISTANCE

1.5-km loop

ELEVATION GAIN

Negligible

DIFFICULTY

The trail is easy but does require being a little sure-footed around some of the rooty sections and can require climbing over dead-fall, depending on the time of year.

SEASON

All season, but wear boots during the wet season to wade across two small streams.

OF SPECIAL INTEREST FOR CHILDREN

The lake can get pleasantly warm during the summer: enough said! An information poster about rough-skinned newts, common around the lake, can add spice to the quest for the

The view from the south shore.

colourful critters, especially in spring. Most kids will be fascinated by the information on the poisonous nature of the newts.

1. Turn right along a broad crushed-gravel trail, crossing a sturdy little handrailed bridge, and wander through a stand of tall, second-growth hemlock. Pause at the information poster on the local salamanders or rough-skinned newts.

2. When you come to a gravel road, a loop road serving several tent sites, turn left (but note the potentially useful outhouses). Within a very short distance, come to a sign simply announcing "Trail" and pointing to a small track. This is the proper beginning of the route around the lake. Soon notice

The docks near the campground and parking area.

occasional grapefruit-sized yellow (and, at some points, red) spots painted on trees. These useful splotches mark the trail for the whole route.

3. Although the trail is well back from the edge of the lake along this section, you do come to two side tracks leading left down to the shore. You don't find any beaches, but you do find pretty views. Children might be intrigued by a little lean-to along the second of these trails. Perhaps the world's smallest island sprouts pretty little trees a short distance into the lake.

4. When you come to a second wet-season stream crossing, you may be greeted not by clear trail ahead but by a confusing pile of fallen trees. The trees are, however, easily scrambled over and, in any case, may be cleared away by the time you visit the trail.

5. The trail climbs slightly then swings left to merge with a broad, level roadbed. Within a few minutes, arrive at some walk-in tent sites. The path to your starting point, a short distance away, is a little vague, especially in the wet season when you must make your way across a squelchy little gully. You may, with small children, find it easiest to walk out to the highway and then walk the short distance back to your vehicle.

CONTACT INFORMATION

BC PARKS
www.env.gov.bc.ca/bcparks

PACIFIC RIM NATIONAL PARK
2040 Pacific Rim Hwy
Ucluelet, BC V0R 3A0
tel: 250.726.3500
fax: 250.726.3520
www.pc.gc.ca/eng/pn-np/bc/
pacificrim/index.aspx

FISHERIES & OCEANS CANADA
(for tides and shellfish closures)
148 Port Augusta St
Comox, BC V9M 3N6
250.339.2031
COMMUNICATIONS BRANCH
200 – 401 Burrard St
Vancouver, BC V6C 3S4
tel: 604.666.0384
fax: 604.666.1847
www.dfo-mpo.gc.ca/index-eng.htm

CAPITAL REGIONAL DISTRICT PARKS
Parks & Environmental Services
490 Atkins Ave
Victoria, BC V9B 2Z8
tel: 250.478.3344
fax: 250.478.5416
www.crd.bc.ca/parks

COMOX VALLEY REGIONAL DISTRICT PARKS AND TRAILS
600 Comox Rd
Courtenay, BC V9N 3P6
tel: 250.334.6000
toll free: 1.800.331.6007
www.comoxvalleyrd.ca/EN/main/
community/parks-trails.html

COWICHAN VALLEY REGIONAL DISTRICT
175 Ingram St
Duncan, BC V9L 1N8
250.746.2500
1.800.665.3955
www.cvrd.bc.ca

REGIONAL DISTRICT OF NANAIMO
Recreation & Parks Services
Oceanside Place
830 W Island Hwy
Parksville, BC V9P 2X4
tel: 250.248.3252
toll free within BC: 1.888.828.2069
fax: 250.248.3159
recparks@rdn.bc.ca
www.rdn.bc.ca

ACKNOWLEDGEMENTS

Thanks to Ann and Marc Abrioux, and Eileen Dombrowski, for help in exploring. Additional thanks to Catrin Brown, for advice and tips.

INDEX

Note: Page numbers in **bold** indicate main routes